THE SCRIBAL REALM OF
DREAMS & VISIONS

LOOK TO SEE WHAT GOD WILL SAY.
- HABAKKUK 2:1

THERESA HARVARD JOHNSON

Theresa Harvard Johnson
950 Eagles Landing Parkway, Ste. 302
Stockbridge, GA 30281

Scripture quotations taken from the Amplified® Bible,
Copyright © 1954, 1958, 1962, 1964, 1965, 1987 by The Lockman Foundation Used by permission.
(www.Lockman.org)

Scriptures taken from the Complete Jewish Bible by David H. Stern. Copyright © 1998. All rights reserved. Used by permission of Messianic Jewish Publishers, 6120 Day Long Lane, Clarksville, MD 21029. www.messianicjewish.net.

Scripture quotations marked (NIV) are taken from the Holy Bible, New International Version®, NIV®. Copyright © 1973, 1978, 1984, 2011 by Biblica, Inc.™ Used by permission of Zondervan. All rights reserved worldwide. www.zondervan.com

Printed in the United States of America.
2016 First Edition
ISBN-10: 1534724443
ISBN-13: 978-1534724440

DEDICATION

For those who LOOK to SEE what God will say...and what answer they will give. ~ *Habakkuk 2:1*

"I am reminded of what we are told in Acts 17:21. The scripture says that the men of Athens spent their time in the city waiting for something new...but also old, proven and scriptural at the same time. The Scribal Realm of Dreams and Visions is such a book. It will change the way you approach the Kingdom in a very powerful and dramatic way. Theresa Harvard Johnson has allowed God to take her deeply into the Chamber of the Scribe and bring out fresh manna. This revelation concerning the scribal realm caused me to take many moments to muse, consider and ponder... as I saw the Kingdom in a new way. There were many instances that prompted me to throw away old thinking and see things in a way I had never seen them before. There were even times when I was struck with amazement as my heart burned and my Spirit was challenged and fed. If you are a seeker who is fully planted on a good foundation, The Scribal Realm of Dreams & Visions will change your life."

~ Chief Apostle Joseph L. Prude, The Cleveland Prophetic Institute

TABLE OF CONTENTS

INTRODUCTION

T his book, *The Scribal Realm of Dreams & Visions*, is specifically for Christ followers who constantly sense an urgency or an extreme "pressure, pull or command" to write, record or demonstrate their Holy Spirit inspired dreams, visions and interpretations.

I believe there are *many* dreamers among the body; but few who take their dreams lives seriously enough to diligently write or record them. As a result, an entire dimension of their relationship with God is lost or should I say, never explored or experienced. There are also second hand casualties to this disobedience – the souls who may be connected to the treasures revealed through the dreamer's obedience to the scribal process. In this unique book, I hope to introduce readers to what I have come to recognize as the "scribal realm" of dreams and visions; the importance of this realm and its distinctions; and answer questions surrounding *why* it is so critical for scribes to awaken to its existence and purpose.

In the beginning of my walk with the Lord, I never considered myself a dreamer. I cannot begin to tell you how *wrong* that self-assessment was. I grew to realize that not only was I a dreamer, but my dream life would prove to be **"the most critical catalyst"** to my connection to scribal ministry.

Let me explain. Shortly after giving my life to the Lord, I went through about three years of intensive prophetic scribal training in the night season with Holy Spirit. Some of these experiences may be very common in your own journey. I was constantly being awakened in the middle of the night with these long streams of poetry and spoken word flowing from me. While I did not really know what was happening, I knew it was the Lord. So I began writing down everything I received through those intimate times by *compulsion* – and have several shelves filled with notebooks to prove it. Eventually, I graduated from receiving poetry and spoken word in the night season to songs and direct prophecies… and pretty soon I was waking up with bible studies, sermons, introductions for state grant applications, ideas for proposals, strategies for my work day in corporate America, content for administrative documents; and all kinds of revelation concerning scripture just emptying from me. Quite simply, I wrote so much during those seasons that I grew to expect it, anticipate it at the same time each night, and soon recognized my experiences as God's preferred way of engaging with me.

As I approached my fourth year in the midst of these experiences, my dream life shifted significantly. I began having some repetitive, unusual detailed dreams of sitting in an ancient, but sturdy old-school, wooden desk wearing a flowing white, chiffon garment. I had ancient parchment before me, several well-used, but elegant inkwells filled with ink. I carried this adorned, personalized stylus and I was copying everything I could see on a huge blackboard directly in front of me. I belonged there. I experienced a level of safety in this place that I cannot even begin to articulate; and I knew that I was in the presence of the Lord.

This desk was positioned on a beautiful, isolated beach directly in the burning sand. My bare feet were nestled in the sand's purity, softness and warmth as the wind blew forcefully against the walls of the huge, pitched white tent encamped around me and breezed into the enclosed space. I was literally experiencing every aspect of this dream… as if I was awake.

It was clear that I was the only student in this setting. I had this inward knowing that this was the only tent on the shore of a massive, beautiful, endless beach. I could see outside the wide, open flaps of the tent's entrance. The sky was bright and clear – like it often is after a summer rain. There was a huge ocean as far as the eyes could see. I could hear the calming currents and see the rolling tides. The dream was so vivid that I would awaken smelling the waters, remembering what the ocean breeze felt like and tasting the saltiness in the air.

The best part of the dream, however, was that I could see a man draped in a white robe from head to toe and clothed in a brilliant light writing carefully on the blackboard. His presence was overwhelming to me. Though there was no visible stylus in His hands, Hebrew characters would rise off the surface of the blackboard like fire with each stroke of his hand, and then take their permanent place on the blackboard. I knew the man writing was Christ; and every now and then, He would turn his head toward me and nod in approval. Then I would wake up... frantically writing pages and pages that would later, unknown to me, become many of the books I am releasing today.

Sometimes I asked myself what would have happened if I had not recorded what I received? How could I have known that one day, Holy Spirit would quicken me to revisit those notes, prophecies and messages and pour revelation concerning them into my heart? Listen, I am not bragging or boasting here. I am presenting you with an earnest testimony of how I got here... to the place of writing *this* book. I am presenting you with an opportunity to question how you "respond to God" in your dream life? I am presenting a case which states: What was taking place in the night season as I slept and in the midst of my open visions gave birth to The Scribal Anointing® in me. Ignoring this aspect of my dream life would have closed the spiritual pipeline that ignited scribal ministry as I have come to understand it.

Today, I know that I have been walking *intentionally* in the scribal realm of dreams and visions for nearly two-decades. Just because there were times when I woke up in the middle of the night to write without the ability to recall a single vision *did not mean* I had not dreamed or been taken up by the Lord. It simply meant that I did not necessarily remember that encounter.

Scribes of the King, could those late night scribal encounters that so many of us have be a deposit from a secret, specific place in the spirit? Could it be that the encounter was so intense that the only thing you could do was wake up and record what you heard or the impression that you received? I may be going too far with this for some believers. Yet, I really believe this is what sometimes happens to those chosen by God to scribe visions, dreams…. the destiny of a people. I have had many Déjà vu type experiences - meaning feeling like I had been at a particular place or point in time before. Then, I heard this in my spirit one day: *"Beloved… you have."*

In **2 Corinthians 12:2-4** (NIV) the Apostle Paul said this about his supernatural experience in the realm of dreams and visions: *"I know a man in Christ who fourteen years ago-- whether in the body I do not know, or out of the body I do not know, **God knows**-- such a man was caught up to the third heaven. And I know how such a man-- **whether in the body or apart from the body I do not know, God knows-- was caught up into Paradise and heard inexpressible words,** which a man is not permitted to speak."*

Let me make this clear: I am not claiming in any way shape or form to be like the Apostle Paul. I am not saying I have all the answers but I do believe God has given me a part! And that part, I choose to share with you. People of God, I have had supernatural experiences after the pattern of great biblical men. I am sure many of you have also. While some may not believe any of what is written in this book, I have to stand like the Apostle Paul and say: *"Only God knows! He is the only one who can stand as a witness to my experiences!"*

I have come to realize that all of my songs, plays, skits, books and book ideas – every single one of them – have come from the scribal realm of dreams and visions. Over the past four years, I've taken the time to hire illustrators to sketch some of the most vivid scenes I have had to go along with the words I was commanded to write. I do not know what I am to do with some of those sketches at the moment; but I know that at the appointed time it will be revealed to me.

My role is simple: Be obedient to my Father.

Today, my dream encounters are primarily with angels. When they appear in my dreams, they always open scrolls in my presence or give me scrolls to carry. In a few of those dreams, I saw myself accept scrolls and then pass them on to others like a baton. Spiritually, I am in place now that I can properly interpret dreams like that.

People of God, do not discount or dismiss the potential of this gift in your spiritual life OR your ability to access this supernatural place! Please know that it is not made available to everyone. If you find yourself drawn into the dream realm, begin asking Holy Spirit how to help you prepare your heart for every encounter from this point forward. You do not have to take the passive approach to your spiritual encounter as most people do. **You can prepare yourself to receive the Lord!** If you hear the COMMAND to scribe what God has given you, do it! The command to write and record is about WAY MORE than the act of writing, demonstration or recording itself… nor does it rest solely on the dream's interpretation. Again, there are hidden treasures in the scribal *process* – not just the interpretation.

1 Thessalonians 5:20 NIV says, *"Do not treat prophecies with contempt but test them all; hold on to what is good…"*

When we ignore our God-centered dream realm, we are treating prophecies with contempt. **The dream realm IS PROPHECY.** It is prophetic ministry. It is revelation. The dream realm provides endless opportunities to grow in the admonition, obedience and the *fear of the Lord*. The dream realm provides powerful exercises in discernment; and tremendous tools for growing and maturing in the things of the Lord.

Listen, I completely understand the tendency to dismiss the supernatural realm of dreams and visions. It's easy to believe dreams and visions are the result of a bad meal, an overactive imagination, subliminal messages from the cares of the day and so forth. In addition, there are people who take this stuff to the extreme and operate out of great mental confusion, manipulation *and* outright abuse. **You can abuse the prophetic! You can misinterpret soulish activity for spiritual encounters.** This is why we are commanded to "test them all" in **1 Thessalonians 5**. But we are NEVER told to dismiss them all! Lying prophets, super-spiritualists, confused dreams filled with the cares of this world... and over the top Pharisees will be with us until Christ returns. We, however, are the discerning ones, and it is our responsibility to sift through the dross.

God said this in **Jeremiah 23:25-26, 32** KJV, *"I have heard what the prophets said, that prophesy lies in my name, saying, I have dreamed, I have dreamed. How long shall this be in the heart of the prophets that prophesy lies? Yea, they are prophets of the deceit of their own heart..."*

"Indeed, I am against those who prophesy false dreams, declares the LORD. They tell them and lead my people astray with their reckless lies, yet I did not send or appoint them. They do not benefit these people in the least, declares the LORD."

These counterfeits and manipulators must not cause us to be paranoid, uncomfortable and suspicious of every dream and dreamer we encounter. They must not stop us from believing that God's best is often hidden in our dreams. It is okay to ask God to help you discern the difference between His truth and a lie! I beg you, do not allow negative experiences to close your mind to revelation in this area.

Also know that this book is specifically about the God-centered dream realm. It is about standing as a beacon of affirmation for scribes who dream-- declaring that your dream realm matters and has significance. **So as I share this revelation, please note that it is taught from the perspective of the Godly dreamer.** What does this mean? It means that I am speaking to sons of God in this book. I am speaking to those who dream within their holy, sanctified and righteous lives. I am speaking to those who "live in Christ" according to **2 Corinthians 5:21**. I am speaking to those who hear and know His voice, and do not pursue the voice of strangers.

Joel 2:28 AMP says, *"And afterward I will pour out My Spirit upon all flesh; and your sons and your daughters shall prophesy, your old men shall dream dreams, your young men shall see visions."*

Each one of us have been given *full access* to the realm of dreams and visions via Holy Spirit. Does this indicate that everyone will dream nightly, have constant intense visions or walk with the Lord in the capacity of a prolific seer? No, it does not. It does indicate that you can expect God to meet you in the dream realm at some point in your life. It means when He does that you must be present for that encounter and prepared to respond.

Before I move into this teaching, I want to clarify five things about this book:

1) It is best used as a study guide and/or *supplement* to an existing, biblically sound teaching, book or course on dreams or visions – especially from a prophetic perspective. It is not intended to be a definitive guide on dreams and visions; rather it is addressing only the scribal focus.

2) The basics of dreams, visions and interpretation are *not* covered here. Any general terms and definitions provided will be basic and geared toward bringing understanding to the "scribal aspect" of dreams and visions.

3) Dream interpretation is not addressed here. I don't want you to be disappointed about this, so I am sharing that fact up front; however, what is presented will be *extremely* helpful in advancing the knowledge and revelation surrounding interpretation.

4) Please remember that this book is specifically for those who are compelled, pulled or drawn to write, record and demonstrate their dreams. In other words, it is for those immersed in scribal ministry. There is a difference between being obligated to scribe your dreams and being commanded or compelled by God to do so.

5) It is an excellent companion for those who are mature in teaching on dreams and visions within schools of Holy Spirit, schools of the prophet, schools of dreams and visions, etc.

In this hour, the Lord is truly releasing His heart to those destined to scribe for Him. It is my prayer that this book, in some way, will significantly impact your life, bring confirmation to your calling and compel you to obey the Father above man.

May the peace and blessings of the Lord and the **Matthew 13:52** scribal anointing continue to overwhelm and overtake you in this season.

Embracing Immersion,

Theresa Harvard Johnson

The Unlikely Scribe

But God chose what the world considers nonsense in order to shame the wise; God chose what the world considers weak in order to shame the strong; and God chose what the world looks down on as common or regards as nothing in order to bring to nothing what the world considers important; so that no one should boast before God.
~ 1 Corinthians 1:27-29

THE PROPHET HABAKKUK

The Prophet Habakkuk might seem like an unlikely candidate to help God's people understand the scribal realm of dreams of visions. After all, he wasn't taken up into the heavens like Ezekiel, Peter and Paul; or given a great mystery to partially reveal and then seal as God's Word like Daniel or John. In fact, he is listed as a minor prophet. He never prophesied directly to anyone and few scholars have ever acknowledged him as a dreamer, or at least one whose life and ministry contributes significantly to dreams and visions. This prophet is remembered best for his dialogue with God in the style of Job or Jonah; his own spiritual quest for answers in the midst of great frustration and confusion; and for gaining a solid response from God to an extremely important burden he carried concerning a serious dilemma facing Judah at the time.

Yet... I am convinced that Habakkuk's name belongs on the wall of great prophets, dreamers and seers; and that his ministry experience in this area, though *considerably* different from other prophets in the bible, adds tremendous insight into what we have learned of the most dramatic and prolific dreamers in the history of scripture.

Let's take a look at some historical information about this prophet.

Habakkuk's tenure as a prophet spanned from c. 609 BC to 598 BC in Judah, around the latter part of the 7th Century.[1] We know from scripture that he was a contemporary of the prophets Nahum, Zephaniah and Jeremiah.[2] He is described as man of vigorous faith and a follower of Israel's traditions. It is from Habakkuk's visions that the Apostle Paul ran with the revelation that the "just shall live by faith" **(Hab. 2:4).** Who would

---

[1] Minor Prophets, *Rose Book of Bible Charts, Maps & Timelines*, Rose Publishing (2005: Torrance, California), p. 12.

[2] David. F. Payne, *Kingdoms of Our Lord,* Wm. B. Eerdmans Press, (1981), p. 249, http://www.biblicalstudies.org.uk/pdf/payne-kingdoms/24.pdf

have imagined that a *minor prophet* would one day inspire such a major New Covenant doctrine? It is truly one of those off-the-beaten-path type of things, especially since Habakkuk never released a single SPOKEN oracle to anyone. Nor is he credited with authoring any other text in the scriptures outside of this book. From a scribal perspective, this is amazing!

Scholars agree that outside of what is revealed about him in scripture, very little documentation has been found that provides information about his life or lineage. However, a popular theory in Rabbinic tradition names him as the son of the Shunammite woman in 2 Kings 4.[3] There is also speculation that he was the son of Joshua of the Tribe of Levi.[4] While there is no clear understanding of the meaning of his name, some scholars agree that it probably means "to embrace."[5] Prophetically speaking, it really fits the man we will come to know in this book, *"The Scribal Realm of Dreams & Visions."* At the end of his discourse, he walked into a completely fresh understanding of God! He also held his individual purpose and destiny in new esteem.

We glean from scripture that Habakkuk encountered first-hand the terrors, sufferings and violence against the people of Judah. His knowledge of their predicament was clearly from the perspective of an eye witness and confirms that his environment was chaotic, stressful, frightening and *full of terror* – which is reflective of his lament in the first two chapters of the book.

One commentary summarized the prophet's plight this way:

> "Habakkuk was perplexed that wickedness, strife and oppression were rampant in Judah but God seemingly did nothing. When told

---

[3] Bible.org, *An Introduction to the Book of Habakkuk,* https://bible.org/article/introduction-book-habakkuk
[4] Ibid.
[5] Bible Study Tools, Quick Reference Dictionary: Habakkuk, http://www.biblestudytools.com/dictionary/habakkuk/

that the Lord was preparing to do something about it through the "ruthless" Babylonians (1:6), his perplexity only intensified: How could God, who is "too pure to look on evil" (1:13), appoint such a nation "to execute judgment" (1:12) on a people "more righteous than themselves" (1:13)?[6]

This prophet, like his contemporaries, walked alone in the midst of his calling and often witnessed *extreme* circumstances and situations. Many who are reading this text now will agree that – in all truth – we have never experienced this type of trauma on an *ongoing and consistent basis, nor at this level.* Witnessing this type of devastation and still walking faithfully with God was the norm for prophets, and all sons for that matter, of the Old Covenant (and New Covenant) whom we glean from. Considering this provides new lenses by which we can view their lives and ministries. Thank God that we have Body ministry in this hour, people we can draw upon to stand with us amid the new design! This doesn't mean that "no one" can identify with this specific prophet, but it does cause us to be mindful of his level of suffering, endurance for the sake of the message of God. Habakkuk's single place of solace was an escape into deep prayer, practicing the presence of God. Our struggle may not be reminiscent of his in present day, but I pray that everyone who reads this can empathize with his plight, identify with his sufferings and allow the lessons learned from his testimony and example to resonate in their hearts.

From the prophet's laments, we learn that he loved God's people, despised their suffering and carried with him a strong burden of intercession, prayer and hope for their deliverance. There is also no question that Habakkuk had a heart for the Lord even though he was tormented by what he saw as God's seemingly non-response to the people's suffering. As a result, he confronts God and proposes this question: "How can God who is just and

---

[6] Biblica, *Introduction from the NIV Study Bible: Habakkuk,* (Zondervan) http://www.biblica.com/es-us/la-biblia/biblia-en-linea/scholar-notes/niv-study-bible/intro-to-habakkuk/

good, who hates evil and cannot look upon it, allow a nation that has greater wickedness than His own people *brutally* overtake them? **(Hab. 1:12-18)"**

What a bold question to ask the Lord, especially in a dispensation when people FEARED God… as in he-is-going-to-kill-me terror, not just reverence. There was VERY little questioning concerning His motives in scripture. But when you consider the dire situation Habakkuk is in; and his inability to provide an answer or solution for the people he was sent to watch over and prophesy to — *it makes perfect sense* for him to present such an argument to our Father. Note that in presenting his argument, there is still a massive level of humility exemplified. In the last part of **Habakkuk 2:2**, the prophet makes it clear that he stands in expectation of being reproved or chastised for his actions. Nevertheless, he stands boldly before God willing to risk it all to have his question answered. This blessed me on two major fronts:

(1) First, I infer here that Habakkuk wanted to serve God without hindrance. That meant that he needed a pure heart. He was willing to risk everything to clear up any possible confusion, assumptions. He recognized that where he was in his own thinking had the potential to skew his relationship with God.

(2) Secondly, Habakkuk realized he had to chase after this particular revelation. So instead of waiting for it to hit him by osmosis, he pursued understanding beyond himself.

In Old Covenant scripture, we are accustomed to seeing God call prophets directly, give them a specific word without them seeking it out and cause them to go to specific nations, people or leaders with that word. Habakkuk's quest was markedly different. I'd go as far as to say that for the prophetic scribe it is **so different** that it causes us to see a need to be more active in our pursuit of revelation. Did God respond to Habakkuk's inquiry? Oh yes, He did! And, He did so in great detail. It revealed a New

Day for the prophets and the people of God's time! We will take a look at that later. It is also here where Habakkuk's scribal connection begins to unfold and take shape in *the scribal realm* of dreams and visions. And this is where we start our journey.

HABAKKUK'S SCRIBAL CONNECTION

Knowing as much as possible about the prophet Habakkuk's background makes all the difference in reading this book, *"The Scribal Realm of Dreams & Visions."* It places his life in context of the scripture and provides an opportunity for his uniqueness to come alive for us. It causes us to see his journey as a prophet from a unique perspective, and perhaps to see glimpses of ourselves through his story. As I wrote sections of this book, I thought about the time he must have spent considering God's decision concerning the people of Judah. In my holy imagination, I pictured the scenarios that may have occupied his thoughts concerning whether or not he would confront God. I even imagined the anguish he must have felt wondering why God had not told him outright WHY the people were suffering. After all, he was indeed God's appointed prophet given charge over this city. Why wouldn't God reveal this to his servant the prophet?

Often when scriptures are read, we do not know the back story that preceded the fruit, the revelation. As a result, we unintentionally see the people of God as characters in a good story, an elaborately written epic, fable or tragedy. Habakkuk was a man just like any other. He was called to do a work – that even now we only have a cameo of through the Bible. We know he was well acquainted with the political uprising in his region; and that he passionately scribed those experiences in a document that somehow managed to transcend time, generations.

Habakkuk was a man chosen by God to be a prophet. He was a man whose contributions have been devalued by modern day scholars because – by page count – his contribution seems small in comparison with the flood of revelation revealed by others. For the prophetic scribe, this is major. We do not always speak in VOLUMES or reach millions by way of audience.

Yet, the message of our hearts (God's heart) is just as valuable as the one whose name everyone knows. One word spoken into the ear of one man, can shift that entire lineage. I often say, *impact* is in the eye of the beholder. God wants this truth to rest deeply **IN** every scribe who identifies with the message in this book.

Habakkuk was categorized as minor… or lesser because of what was seen with the natural eye… leaving a stigma that has trailed him and eleven other prophets like him through the centuries. Yet, scholars have accredited him as being a "literary genius" – especially in the area of poetry.[7] He, however, never had an opportunity to know this because thousands of years separate his lifetime from ours. His expertly crafted dialogue and elaborate poems are meditated upon as revelation from God even to this day. People whom he would never have imagined are continuously drawing wisdom, knowledge and understanding from his experiences, recorded oracles and prayers. He became known anyway…. not by the ways of men, but by the ways and will of God. When God makes you famous… it lasts beyond a single generation. This is why we do not have to worry about who receives his message in us, as long as we are recognized and sent by the King.

Scribes, God already has had the last say.

In addition, we also know that Habakkuk was highly educated. Somewhere, in the course of his life Habakkuk went to school. Where ever he studied, he had great freedom to develop his own powerful voice and sound. Reading and writing was not common among people in biblical times. To some degree it also indicates that he may have come from a lineage of great wealth or at least had access to the people who could afford to give him such an education. In consideration of the depth of his poetic genius, we can also conclude that he may have had training in rhetoric,

---

[7] Leland Ryken, James C. Wilhoit, Tremper Longman III. Dictionary of Biblical Imagery, *Book of Habakkuk* (1998: Downers Grove), Inter-Varsity Press, p. 357-358.

public speaking or was heavily influenced by it. It is **obvious** that he had his own, unique poetic style – which infers that he was a frequent writer, poet and psalmist – especially when we consider the prayer he sang in **Habakkuk 3**. In some translations, the preceding words to the prayer states that it should be song to "wild and crazy music." I cannot begin to describe the level of joy I had when I read this! All I could think of was how this seemingly solemn prophet knew how to break-loose and give God *crazy* praise for not only answering his inquiry... but for giving him understanding! He released irrational praise like King David. Why is this so significant? It's significant because Habakkuk is not shouting and dancing because God "changed the situation." In fact, you will learn that the situation will become even more dire and desperate for the people of Judah following this oracle. Habakkuk is shouting because the answer he sought *fortified and rooted him* in what he had known to be true about God all along!

Habakkuk's dream realm allowed him to touch incomprehensible joy and strength. The kind that pushes souls to finish the race set before them. Also note the scriptures reveal that: (1) Habakkuk's oracles were written by **command**; (2) Habakkuk's oracles were never delivered to any specific person or audience directly; (3) Habakkuk never spoke the oracles out loud to anyone; and (4) Habakkuk's oracles were assigned to "heralds or runners" – those with the capacity to catch the vision and propel it. He was never given any specific instruction to go and publish the oracles himself. In fact, the inference in **Hab. 2:1-3** is that God would publish the oracles by divine design.

These four points illustrate that the prophet Habakkuk's assignment was linked to a "scribal dimension" of **writing and publishing** in the dream realm. He wrote what God said, published it with the intent of preservation... and left its distribution in the hands of God. Even without digging any further at this point, his *scribal* connection is very clear: God explicitly wanted the treasures drawn from Habakkuk's visions recorded, published and distributed. For the present day "prophetic" scribe, this means that we should EXPECT God to command us to record and write from the realm of dreams and visions.

Habakkuk's loudest and most powerful voice as a prophet travelled from his stylus and inkwell to parchment. Is this a reflection of your journey as well? After receiving the command to write the message, this prophetic scribe was tasked with preparing and positioning the message for mass distribution across time and through thousands of generations! His ministry as a prophetic scribe was **distinctly *literary*,** meaning intentionally released AND presented in a written format for physical distribution on paper – with the intent to be read and sealed into the hearts of men. **We must remind ourselves... again that it does not seem to be God's desire for Habakkuk to represent or present the message himself.** While this is clearly not the case for everyone, the implications here are obvious. As far as God was concerned, Habakkuk was effective in completing His assignment "as is."

Scribes, I hope you catch that.

Habakkuk's humility before God is astounding! The thought of not receiving recognition for one's labor would be too much to bare for most scribes! His motives, however, are clearly centered on God... and his amazing celebration was completely selfless. It didn't matter to him whether he was the one to deliver the oracle or not. Oh if our hearts were rent for a posture such as this.

I know personally that we can spend a great deal of time focusing on representing or carrying what God gives us as scribes. I know that we can long for and covet things others have or that we think we deserve – like recognition, the opportunity to deliver the message ourselves, fame, etc. I've been there, done that... repented for it. Even now, I seek to make sure I stay in a submitted place of longing for Him, not His hand. For many of us… that comes with a great deal of breaking and bending into the Father's will. What if you were never meant to do anything more than write the message and make it available in a published form? What if attempts to break your scribal project through into mass markets failed for this very reason? Would it be enough for you to simply have completed the assignment? This is a critical question in this hour. The truth is, not all of the books we write, the plays we produce, the poetry we recite, the novels we publish, etc. will reach masses of people. Perhaps that scribal project is meant to explode in the ears of a future generation? What if that project was only assigned for a remnant? Prophetic scribes, this line of questioning and thinking is a game changer. It takes selfishness out the equation and places God's will at the center. Habakkuk teaches us this valuable lesson. (By no means, however, am I throwing off on being a best seller! This is good… but we do need to address the other side of it as well.)

Psalm 143:10 AMP, *"Teach me to do Your will [so that I may please You], For You are my God; Let Your good Spirit lead me on level ground."*

John 4:34 CJB, *"Yeshua said to them, my food is to do what the one who sent me wants and to bring his work to completion."*

Psalm 84:10 KJV, *"For a day in thy courts is better than a thousand. I had rather be a doorkeeper in the house of my God, than to dwell in the tents of wickedness."*

For the present day scribe who is pressured or compelled to record what God releases to them, this is **contemplative** insight for you to explore.

HE SAW THE ORACLE

Let's take a look at Habakkuk's journey into the dream realm. **Habakkuk 1:1** AMP says, ***"The oracle** (a burdensome message—a pronouncement from God) **which Habakkuk the prophet SAW."*** Note that nearly all formal bible translations agree that the last word of this verse is "SAW," as in something has been seen or perceived with the eyes – spiritual or natural. Other translations also use the word "SEE" which has the same basic connotation. The Hebrew lexicon has an additional note which defines the use of this word as "to see as a *seer* in the ecstatic (blissful, euphoric) state."

Immediately, we are introduced to Habakkuk as he enters a vision (a dream while wide awake). Without question, we know that this encounter took place within the presence of the Lord simply by following the dialogue in **vs. 2-11**. We can conclude that this vision is not typical when compared to the elaborate and demonstrative visions we read about from known biblical dreamers because it simply says he "saw" the oracle. Nothing else is described so that if forms definitive images. It is also important to note that Habakkuk was a prophet who operated primarily *as a seer* (**1 Samuel 9:9**). A seer, in biblical times, was a prophet who prophesied and discerned primarily out of pictures, visions and perceptions. For me, this is a good basic definition… but I also see a seer as one who exists spiritually in a constant "dream state" as it relates to their spiritual connection to God. So when the scripture says, the prophet SAW… it literally means that he SAW in the spirit realm – not the natural. This understanding leads us to the most critical question of our text: "What exactly did Habakkuk see?"

Listen, please do not think that I am out of my mind or stretching scripture when I pose this next question in conjunction with the one above: "Could Habakkuk have actually visualized a written message and recorded it?" There are strong biblical connections and texts supporting the possibility that this prophet **SAW WORDS**. I realize now that the chronicles of the dreamers of the Bible are constantly challenging us in how we consider our dream state.

For those who truly embrace the supernatural reality of God, we understand the dream realm beyond allegory and beyond the viewpoint that only the biblical characters who actual lived in the scriptures experienced these types of encounters. We interpret it with the same supernatural

14

comprehension that allows us to conceptualize the reality of angels, demons, translation, transfiguration, resurrection, miracles, signs and wonders. We also embrace biblical truths relating to dreams and visions in which God chooses to communicate with his people by way of impressions, images or movie-like scripts played out in great detail in the style of Zephaniah, Joseph, Ezekiel, Isaiah or Daniel. We are also accepting dreams and visions from the perspective of quick flashes or trances like those of the apostles Peter, Paul and John. I want to also challenge you to consider the unusual dream connection with Paul and Ananias. There is even an understanding of dream encounters with God's presence in which he speaks directly in the hearing of His people in night visions or open visions; and intense encounters with angels. In other words, receiving the "voice of God" for numerous people of the Bible was also equated to the experiencing a dream or vision. An excellent example of this was when Samuel was resting in his bed and he heard the Lord call him forth **(1 Samuel 3)**. Scribes, I am asking you again: "WHAT did Habakkuk see? Is it possible that Habakkuk **saw** literal words?" From a revelatory perspective, I believe he did!

Listen, we are going to explore this. First, let us examine the foundation scripture for *"The Scribal Realm of Dreams & Visions."*

Habakkuk 2:1-3 NIV reads, *"I will stand at my watch and station myself on the ramparts. I will **'LOOK-TO-SEE'** what **'HE-WILL-SAY'** to me, and what answer I am to give to this complaint. Then the Lord replied:*

"Write down the revelation and make it plain on tablets so that a herald may run with it. For the revelation awaits an appointed time; it speaks of the end and will not prove false. Though it linger, wait for it; it will certainly come and will not delay."

Throughout my life in Christ this passage of scripture has always been the "go to passage" for positioning one's self in prayer for the purpose of casting visions for business plans, life goals, creating your best life and so forth. **The truth is:** That perspective is a far cry from the author's intent.

These passages came on the heels of a suffering prophet who desperately needed to understand why a loving God was allowing such destruction to come to a people whom He claimed to love. In a drastic attempt to understand how God could allow or cause this, the prophet repositioned himself as a watchmen or intercessor over this concern and the people's plight. So when Habakkuk declares that he is *looking-to-see*, the prophet is actually looking for understanding **for this SPECIFIC** situation. Habakkuk wanted God to answer his question. Period. When God declares that he is to write the vision and make it plain, he is referencing the recording of **THIS specific oracle.** Casting a vision for a marketing plan or a great business idea is the furthest thing from this prophet's mind and heart. This was a weighty vision – dug out from a guttural place in the realm of the spirit… dealing with a life and death situation, a situation centered on the eternal destination of the souls of the people of God.

Further, the prophet is experiencing the same kind of open vision he experienced in **Hab. 1:1.** This time, however, he clearly states that he is **"LOOKING-TO-SEE"** what God **"WILL-SAY"** to him.

In the world of theology, there is no disagreement that Habakkuk was standing on his rampart – a wall, watchtower, embankment or barricade - in expectation of an open vision. In biblical times, this rampart was a literal *physical* location. Some scholars suggest that his efforts **to see** may have involved a combination of an open vision as well as an inward revelation or knowing what God spoke. Both are common to the dream realm and to prophecy. Habakkuk, however, is very specific in stating that he was *looking* for *the oracle* of God with his eyes. And, he saw it.

To answer the initial question: Could Habakkuk have seen the words of God? I believe that answer is yes. It is possible that Habakkuk was "seeing a stream of words" or "reading from a heavenly scroll" released directly to him." Let me say this again. It is possible that this prophet literally SAW the WRITTEN WORD OF GOD through a vision. His perception in the realm of dreams and visions could be one in which **"HE SEES WORDS"** and **"HE WRITES OR RECORDS WHAT HE SEES AT GOD'S COMMAND."**

I shared aspects of my testimony in the introduction of this book. I have experienced seeing literal words and receiving scrolls in my dreams and visions. Anyone who knows me personally will agree that I am not a "spooky" or "hyper-spiritual" believer. You will RARELY here me begin a sentence with the religious ring "God showed me this or God showed me that" or end a conversation with "if God releases me to do this or if he releases me to do that." I have learned that people listen and receive better when we just talk to them and share without all the pomp and circumstance. In fact, I rarely discuss my supernatural experiences in the realm of dreams and visions because – quite frankly – very few people actually take this aspect of their lives – much less that of anyone else's - seriously enough to believe; and those who choose to share often fail to release their experiences or revelations in a graceful or humble way. As a result, they find themselves mocked, ignored, looked at sideways or even avoided by brethren. In embracing my understanding of the supernatural, I do so with grace – keeping things often between myself and God unless disclosure is necessary and relevant. For me, this book is that specific platform. It is my prayer that you find yours and treat the realm of dreams, visions and all things supernatural with apostolic grace and care.

My "process" in the midst of these experiences are often private. This book is a huge jump for me. I am literally putting myself out there. As with any of our experiences in the supernatural, we often have no firm witness to the truth of these things except the witness of God himself!

David said this in **Psalm 19:4** NIV, *"May these WORDS of my mouth and this MEDITATION of my heart be pleasing in <u>YOUR SIGHT, LORD</u>, my Rock and my Redeemer."* Note that David is declaring that God is able to **SEE** the **WORDS** he speaks out loud. He also states that the meditation of his heart becomes **WORDS** to God.

Hebrews 4:13 NIV says, *"Nothing in all creation is hidden from God's SIGHT..."* Note here that EVERYTHING is VISIBLE to God. Really grasp hold of this. The word sight here, like SAW in **Habakkuk 2** encompasses all areas and dimensions of sight both in the natural and the spirit. It truly means God sees everything.

Daniel 5:5 CJB says, *"Suddenly, **the fingers of a human hand appeared <u>and began writing</u>** on the plaster of the palace wall by the lamp stand."*

When read in context, you will learn that an unrighteous king is having a VISION OF WORDS from the dream realm being revealed on a wall through handwriting.

The prophet Zechariah **<u>SAW</u>** a flying scroll in his open vision, and literally **<u>READ</u>** what was on the front and back of it **(Zech. 5:1-3)**. The prophecy that followed contained critical insight into the content of the scroll.

These passages undeniably illustrate examples of **SEEING WORDS** through dreams and visions. Then, we must consider that everything created by God began with WORDS and that everything that ended, also ended with Words! Christ is alpha and omega.

While we will not go in-depth into the Book of Revelation, it is important to note that the apostle John is a New Covenant example of a scribal apostle – one who was compelled to write and record **(the Gospel of John and I, II and III John)**; and who was commanded to write the Revelation of Jesus Christ. While he did not "see words" per se; he was commanded to write

18

what HE SAW by way of an elaborate and critical open vision. The seal of this understanding can be found in the opening chapter. **Revelation 1:19** CJB says, *"So WRITE down what you SEE, both what is now, and what will happen afterwards."*

Scribes, there are many of you right now who are reading this… and have been looked upon as crazy, unstable, super spiritual, etc. because very few people have BELIEVED that God speaks to you this way. Who would think that someone SEES words? Let me tell you, I do. I believe you… because God speaks to me this way. Habakkuk saw Words (**Habakkuk 1:1, Habakkuk 2:2**). We also know that his dream life included seeing images and pictures (**Habakkuk 3:10**); and he also heard the sound of God approaching (**Habakkuk 3:15-16**).

Previously, I shared my experiences about being in Christ's classroom along a beach. In this experience, I saw words being illuminated and written on a chalk board in my presence. I have also had other experiences in my dreams including receiving new writing instruments, seeing scrolls unfold in heaven, receiving scrolls from angels and having scrolls opened before me. There is NOTHING in the scripture that tells us that God can only speak to us in one single way.

If we can accept that Ezekiel **ate scrolls** and found them to **taste like honey** during his supernatural experiences in the dream realm, why do we think God cannot meet us with similar experiences through Holy Spirit? I have had dream encounters in which my spiritual senses came alive – and I promise you, I was in the presence of God… not in a demonic encounter or in the presence of a familiar spirit. Let this passage of scripture encourage you. **Numbers 12: 6** CJB says, *"He said, "Listen to what I say: when there is a prophet among you, I, Adonai, **make myself known to him in a vision, I speak with him in a dream.**"*

Those who SEE WORDS see them because they exist and live in the SCRIBAL REALM of visions and dreams. They **SEE** WORDS because their function in the dream realm is to WRITE, DEMONSTRATE and/or RECORD "THE WORDS" they see. If the Lord can appoint angels as scribes to record the supernatural goings on in Heaven and to keep Heaven's library, surely He can use us to capture the supernatural goings-on in earth through our dreams and visions and build a library here as well.

WRITING OR RECORDING

Believe it or not, writing and recording are not the same thing. Though they are very close in meaning there are some distinct differences that we need to understand – especially as scribes. Briefly, I would like to distinguish between the two for the purpose of our discussion here.

Writing is defined as the "activity or skill of writing"[8] in which words, thoughts or ideas are composed as text for the purpose of increasing knowledge and guaranteeing comprehension. Encyclopedia.com supports this definition as well. It defines writing as "the activity or skill of marking coherent words on paper and composing text"[9] with a specific interest in style – including penmanship, lettering, etc.

Writing is a discipline, an art form that is dependent upon skill and style. One who writes generally has great concern about how the message is presented; and the presentation is subjective to the spirit of the writer. In this sense, we are referencing the renewed, Godly spirit of the writer. For example, this book that I am writing now is inspired by God and is a revelation of what He has given me on this subject. However, as you read

---

[8] Oxford Dictionaries Online, Writing,
http://www.oxforddictionaries.com/definition/english/writing
[9] Encyclopedia.com, Writing,
http://www.encyclopedia.com/utility/printdocument.aspx?id=1O999:writing

it… you are also gaining insight into my unique voice, writing style and personality. **I am *writing* a book, not recording one.**

Daniel 7:1 AMP says, *"In the first year of Belshazzar king of Babylon Daniel had a dream and visions appeared in his mind as he lay on his bed; then <u>he wrote the dream down</u> and related <u>a summary</u> of it."*

Daniel's process here clearly shows a "writing process," not the act of recording alone. Recording, though it can also be a *form* of writing, has some unique distinctions. For example, recording can be as simple as dictation – which has no regard for style or a person's specific way of saying things. Its goal is to simply make a record of what is seen or heard. Period. I can make a grocery list right now – that is not writing (as in being a writer), it is recording. Another way of viewing this is from the perspective of a video camera. You simply point the camera at a scene and hit record – as is. Recording is defined as "making an official record of."[10] It is relaying the "facts" as in who, what, when, where and how for the sole purpose of making a permanent record. It does not necessary require any specific skill set other than spelling and putting legible text on paper. It is not dependent on anything other than an ability to capture what is presented. Copying from another copy is also an example of recording. It is also viewed as "the *practice* of one who records."[11] In truth, a writer could also be a recorder and recorder could also be someone who writes. Yet, a recorder could also be someone who DOES NOT WRITE but simply records. This is critical because many people believe that scribes must be called as "writers" or that all scribes are "writers." This is simply NOT true. For example, people who input numbers in ledgers or update databases are recorders.

---

[10] Oxford Dictionaries Online, Recording,
http://www.oxforddictionaries.com/us/definition/american_english/recording.
[11] Encyclopedia.com, Recording,
http://www.dictionary.com/browse/recording

According to **Habakkuk 2:2**, this prophet was a "writer" not a recorder. Did God release an oracle to him? Yes, he did. But he did not simply tell him to record it. He said, **WRITE** it. This completely changes how we understand writing. Take a look at this verse in the AMP: *"**Write down** the revelation **and make it plain on tablets** so that a herald may run with it."*

Note that Habakkuk the prophet was GIVEN PERMISSION by God to not simply RECORD WHAT GOD SAID – but to use his skill as a writer to make it EASILY UNDERSTOOD. The phrase "make it plain" indicates this. Habakkuk was challenged in this moment with an apostolic task – he had to bring the Word of God which he SAW from the dream realm into a place of understanding in the EARTH REALM. Remember, he had authority to do this for the audience assigned to the message. In the world system, we might look at this from the perspective of a ghost writer – one who writes AS IF they are the original author. In the course of my employment over the years, I have served in this capacity with authors. Listen, I don't want anyone to get what I am saying twisted. So I want to explain this very well.

The capacity in which Habakkuk wrote was not one in which "he wrote what he wanted to say" or "put his own spin on things." He wrote as one who was IMMERSED in the will of His Father. He wrote as one who understood the HEART of His Father, and WHO DESIRED to convey the message in words with the tenor and the intent in which HE KNEW the Father was speaking. Religion will not fully assimilate this revelation. The best example of this can be found in the life of Christ when He reminds us that he said only what the Father said and did only what He saw the Father do. He didn't always use the Father's exact words, but he definitely conveyed the Father's complete will and heart. So while the "idea" of a ghost writer is present; Habakkuk is releasing this direct oracle with unshakable and unquestionable authority in the Spirit. Period. It is imperative that whoever reads this section of the book… take these truths to heart. By no means should anyone walk away from this understanding thinking that this prophet "wrote what he wanted to write." This simply was not the case. It did mean that he had developed a relationship of trust with God in which he represented Him well before the people, with full liberty to speak on His behalf with this specific message. Remember, a prophet of God is *eternally* the mouthpiece of God. As a prophetic scribe, this truth applies to you as well. Sometimes, God will give a prophetic scribe this kind of trust in his or her area of authority. There are also times in which God will require word-for-word dictation – which is a form of recording. That is fine as well. Let's go further.

In many dreams and visions classes, there are numerous assumptions made about "writing and recording" dreams. It is critical that we really make a distinction between writing and recording dreams out of obligation or necessity; AND writing and recording a dream based on one's office or calling as a scribe. **There is a HUGE difference.** As a master scribe, I found this to be a place of GRAVE ERROR among the people of God. You see, there are many people who write down their dreams for the purpose of remembering it, going back to reference it or for the purpose of gaining interpretive insight now or later. This is good. I encourage it... but it is *not*... and I repeat *it is not* necessarily a scribal function they are performing as a "called scribe of God."

A person functioning as a prophetic scribe will record or write down their dreams because it is an "urgent command" to do so. They operate from **a compelled place**, in the same manner that a prophet operates when a prophecy is ready to be released. Jeremiah described the latter as being like FIRE shut up in his bones that he could no longer contain. I am pretty sure most people who record their dreams do not have "that kind" of urgency. Most people record their dreams out of duty, necessity. They feel they need to or have to do it. All in all, there is absolutely no prophetic pull to do so whatsoever. Again, this difference is critical in distinguishing between the "calling and office of the scribe" under "The Scribal Anointing®" which is rooted in the urgency to record, write or demonstrate something our Father commands to be released in the earth; and our *personal desire* or obligation to write or record something we can reference or look at it later. While both are indeed valuable, the "calling" has an intentional, ordered outcome aligned with a specific mandate that is beyond any individual.

RECORDING AS ILLUSTRATION & PHOTOGRAPHY

I cannot talk about the ministry of the recorder without addressing the *scribal* aspect of "illustration." Illustration for the prophetic scribe is a form of recording and storytelling. The most basic way to define this type of recording is to consider it from a journalistic perspective: The act of clarifying or explaining something pictorially – whether through photography or drawing that "describes" what has, will or is currently taking place. It can be through drawing, painting, photography or even videography (silent or with sound).

Not many people know this, but I am also a well-rounded artist. I spent several years studying photography in college and once owned a dark room. Old school photography was my heart. I enjoyed developing in the dark room and gained quite a reputation for that passion back in college. That's how serious I was about my craft. At one time, I majored in art in college – thinking that I would spend the rest of my life teaching others to love art and history. I even won the coveted title of Ms. Art Club during my sophomore year. Ironically, my love for writing (especially poetry and short stories) superseded my passion for drawing in charcoal and pastels. After graduating, I became a full-time sleuth! I worked in the industry as a professional journalist in some capacity for nearly two decades. It wasn't until I began digging into "prophetic" scribal ministry that I realized my love for art and my love for writing were divinely connected.

We live in a world in which we are constantly separating things – dividing and splitting stuff up. So much so that in the midst of the congregation we have all but destroyed the relationship between "writing and art." It's become so fragmented that both are undervalued and appreciated in its purest forms... and seldom seen as an avenue for pure ministry. To see this relationship up close and personally, all we have to do is study the beauty of calligraphy, penmanship and lettering. It is easy to see – through these lenses – how writing can be considered art.

Father said this to me one day: *"Beloved, even my ancient text was symbols engraved on stone, not written letters."* While this may not be a monumental revelation for most prophetic people, it was for me. After some intensive research, I realized that ancient Hebrew wasn't lettering at all in the sense that we understand the alphabet today. Rather, it was a combination of some amazing symbols that when understood individually or as a group conveyed a massive amount of meaning – something letters in and of themselves could never do. The letter "a" in our culture is just the letter "a" – nothing more, nothing less. The first character of the Hebrew alphabet is "alef" and its symbolism is endless. Historically, writing began with beautifully crafted images and symbols - not with letters. People told stories by "illustrating them" on walls in caves, on bricks, clay tablets and stones... even on their bodies. They carved out scenes or depictions from their lives on rock, wood and animal skin. It was how they "told their stories" in addition to oral tradition which often pointed right back to picture stories. Powerful, isn't it!

Remember, recorders are like the "ultimate preservationists." They do what they do for the purpose of making a record. It's only natural that some scribes exit the dream realm not only with commands to pen lettering, but to also "sketch out visual plans" or "recreate certain scenes" that need to be preserved. In some instances, I have had to employ an illustrator to get the ideas and concepts from me that the Lord *urgently commanded* that I bring forth. (From the perspective of playwrights, poets, script writers, etc., I address this in more detail in my book "Literary Evangelism: Beyond the Open Mic.") For those who sketch from the office of the recorder, there is a "clear message" that the Lord desires to convey.

Let me clarify this further: The office of a recorder will have a direct, specific message that is being conveyed to those who *see* it. For example, a photo journalist who is prophetic might cover war stories. Depending on the image, a specific message is being conveyed like the depth of "suffering amid a particular people group" and the need for "relief of certain types of suffering." If that photographer has an eye for children, then the message would convey the burden for children. The visual artist who creates subjectively will lean more to the art piece being interpreted in multiple ways by the eye of the beholder. While all art is subjective to some degree, they will lean more into this subjectivity than a recorder would. Often times, prophetic artists in this arena will want you to "tell them" what you see; where as a recorder generally presents concrete facts through imagery.

The prophetic artist who is a RECORDER walking in the office of a scribe will lean toward producing that "definitive" message that they "know" must be told. The image presented on the next page is from a vision. It only captures an aspect of the vision… but it was the image I was instructed to bring forth concerning myself alongside a prophecy that was delivered with it. In brief, the message was that I would write many books as a master scribe. Father uses this image to encourage me when I find my strength waning in this area of ministry. I want you to know that you can bring imagery from your dreams to any medium God releases! While I can sketch and draw, I often hire illustrators due to time constraints.

Remember: You are STILL the recorder if you do this. Was not Jeremiah a scribal prophet? God asked him to write down prophecies and distribute them. He did, but *he used his own hired scribe* to record what he spoke.

When I was in Ohio three years ago during a Scribal College, I received a sketch of myself from a prophet in the audience who was "compelled" to convey what she saw in the spirit. I was overwhelmingly blessed! She was "seeing me" in the Spirit as I taught and RECORDING what she saw as I ministered to the people.

She reminded me of a court artist, except her court room was in the scribal realm of dreams and visions – as they are always followed by prophecy and prophetic insight. Could this be you? Are you walking it out AND GROWING in revelation, understanding of your call? Is the Lord requiring you to unify His people through such a gift? One of the leading court artists in the country, Arthur Lien, wrote this on his website:

> "I've been sketching the courts since 1976, and for most of that time the U.S. Supreme Court has been my regular beat. I've been working almost exclusively for NBC News since 1980. Courtroom sketching is a form of visual journalism or reportage drawing that is slowly dying out. Where once upon a time news organization each had their own artist covering a story, today a

"pool" artist often sketches for all. It is a demanding and stressful discipline where the drawing is often done directly and under tight deadline."[12]

After reading this the first time, I heard Father say: *"I am raising up new court artists. Those who report from the court house of heaven."* Scribes, let Him raise you up! If you have neglected your calling to bring your visions and dreams to life in this capacity, repent… and begin again.

PROPHETIC SCRIBES & SCRIBAL PROPHETS

I believe we have done an excellent job of establishing Habakkuk's scribal connection so far. No one can dispute that His encounter with God was one of a scribal nature upon closer examination of the scriptures.

Earlier, we considered the fact that (1) all of his oracles were written; (2) none of his oracles were delivered to a specific audience by him directly but sent in written form; (3) he never spoke his oracles out loud to anyone; and (4) his oracles were assigned to "heralds or runners" at God's command, meaning they were meant to be continuously published by those who had a passion for what God had spoken. Habakkuk's oracles represented God's desire to see this particular word preserved and protected.

Let me pause right here for a moment and share this biblical truth: The very nature of scribal ministry in antiquity is to PROTECT & PRESERVE the Word of God. So if you are a prophetic scribe (which we will clarify later), then the core of your calling is to preserve the Word of God… both literally and figuratively. Our core purpose is to make sure that His purpose and intent is never, ever lost. A person without this desire at

---

[12] Courtartist.com: Going Where Cameras Cannot, http://courtartist.com/about

the root of their calling could *never* be defined as a scribe of the King or a prophetic scribe. Now, let's continue with our topic.

For the period in which Habakkuk lived, these oracles provided answers to one of the most critical questions of his time: *"How can a God who fiercely loves His sons allow such a barbaric people, more evil than they are to overtake them?"* God's response was one in which He explained his nature to Habakkuk. He literally answered a question men have held in their hearts for ages: "If God really loves us, then how can He allow bad things to happen?" I used to ask this question often! Can you imagine how important the answer was to the people at that time who found themselves in such deep spiritual warfare? Just think about it. This CRITICAL question was answered thousands of years ago! And it is still one of the most sought after questions posed about God today. And the answer, well… it hasn't changed one single bit.

There is also another powerful revelation that burns in the background of this scenario. Habakkuk taught us that we can BOLDLY approach God with our questions. Remember, he did this in a time when the fear of God was more like TERROR… not just reverential fear. People understood that if you crossed God, so to speak, the ground might open and swallow you in it. Or, you could end up zapped like Nadab and Abihu. Lightening really did strike them.

God endured with Habakkuk. He honored His prophet, and honored His people – even in their rebellion with an answer to their "watchman" who took a chance and stood in the gap for them. Talk about taking command, walking in authority, seeking answers for yourself and on behalf of others. **This prophet went to great extreme to SEEK and SEE the truth.** Without this press, this truth about God might not have been revealed so plainly. In light of this, we must ask ourselves: What does our prayer life look like? How much seeking are we really doing through intercession and meditation to obtain answers to tough spiritual questions?

The scribal activity in Habakkuk's life is indicative of the foundations of prophetic scribal ministry as we teach them within the Voices of Christ Apostolic Prophetic School of the Scribe. In simple terms, a prophetic scribe is a son of God walking in the office of a scribe, functioning in the capacity of scribes of old (as it relates to their ministry activities) in administrative, instructional and/or creative dimensions for the sole purpose of unifying, strengthening and building the congregation.

Let's read through this excerpt from my book, *"The Scribal Anointing: Scribes Instructed in the Kingdom of Heaven."* It provides a foundation for understanding the prophetic scribe and defining the scribal prophet. It relays the foundation scripture we use to unveil and reveal the heart of scribal ministry in the earth. I believe after reading it, you will have a better insight into the heart of a prophetic scribe.

> **"Matthew 13:52** KJV states*: "Therefore every **scribe instructed** concerning **the Kingdom of Heaven** is **like a householder** who **brings out of his treasure** things **new and old**.*

> "Now take a look at this same scripture below. The bolded and underlined words above have been replaced with their Greek definitions to bring greater understanding.

> *"Therefore every **writer, secretary or recorder who has become a disciple to follow [God's] precepts and instructions** concerning the **heart and mind of God** is like a **master of the house or owner** who **leads out or brings forth** of his **kingly, regal storehouse** things **uncommon, of a new kind or fresh** and **from an earlier time**.*

> "God is saying that every writer, secretary or recorder who has purposed in his heart to follow Christ by living the Word and obeying the Word is a master of his own house! This means that these scribes have made the right choices concerning their walk with the Lord and have denied the desires of the flesh. As a result, the scribes will lead and bring forth wisdom, revelation, knowledge and understanding concerning the word of God that is uncommon and fresh, and from the times that have passed.

"**This is The Scribal Anointing!** It walking out your ministry according to Father's original intent and purposes as revealed here! We are prophetic TREASURE HUNTERS who are revealing the heart and mind of God through our scribal gifts! Please grasp this...we are not revealing OUR minds, but HIS mind!" [13]

"I can't help but encourage you to meditate on this excerpt a while longer. Really ask Holy Spirit to help you develop a deeper understanding of what it means to be a prophetic scribe who walks in The Scribal Anointing®. In the scripture itself, make a mental note of the following phrase: "...*leads out or brings forth of his kingly, regal storehouse.*" You will definitely see this phrase again. Also pay attention to the following declaration from the text: **"We are prophetic TREASURE HUNTERS who are revealing God's heart and mind through our scribal gifts!"** [14]

Prophetic scribes are those who are "instructed" in the heart of God, the way of the Kingdom and who walk it out fully. Now, with a brief explanation of The Scribal Anointing® I am ready to define the scribal prophet. This definition is taken directly from my book, *Signs of a Scribal Prophet.* It reads:

"A scribal prophet is indeed a prophet called and sent by God to operate fully in his or her **Ephesians 4:11** office for the purpose of equipping the Body and maturing the saints. However, the scribal prophet *is not* a separate or different gift from the prophet. Rather, the distinction rests in this simple truth: *This particular prophet-type is **compelled and commanded** to administrate his or her ministry primarily through unique scribal activity.* In other words, prophetic scribal ministry has become God's preferred vehicle through which He administrates the office of the prophet in this person's life. Listen, it does not limit the prophet to *only* operating scribally. There are no boxes here that we can lock God's people inside. However, the scribal prophet will fully function as a prophet as many of us have become accustomed to in this present time of the church AND they will fully

---

[13] Theresa Harvard Johnson, "The Scribal Anointing: Scribes Instructed in the Kingdom of Heaven," (2007: Higher Ground Publishing), p. 27.
[14] Ibid.

function in a scribal capacity." [15]

This totally fits Habakkuk. One of the greatest lessons you can take away is this: God deliberately chose Habakkuk to record this message. If this was a deliberate action on the part of God, how much more deliberate is He with you – whether or not you are an **Ephesians 4:11** prophetic scribe? Listen, you were chosen to deliver whatever message HE placed in you. I pray that all of Father's scribes who are asleep would awaken from their slumber... and recognize the power of God working in them to impact and influence His Kingdom.

HABAKKUK'S AUTHORITY

It is indeed true that God has no respecter of persons. But among His great nation, He gives each son individual assignments that strengthen His corporate destiny and purpose – *that of reconciliation.* There will never, *ever* be a higher agenda than reconciling men in the earth realm. Along with our assignment come a measure of governance that we mature into and embrace. While there is no background information available, we know that Habakkuk tapped into that place of governance or authority specifically set aside for *him.* How do we know this? We know from the evidence:

- Habakkuk knew who he was in God. **(Habakkuk 2:1)**

- Habakkuk was mature in his calling. **(Habakkuk 1-2)**

- Habakkuk freely and boldly questioned God and God responded. **(Habakkuk 1-2).**

---

[15] Theresa Harvard Johnson. *Signs of a Scribal Prophet,* (2015: Stockbridge), The Book Patch, p. ii.

- Habakkuk recognized his seat of authority as a prophet **(Habakkuk 2:1)**.

- Habakkuk had instant access to the supernatural realm of dreams and visions, and what was inside. **(Habakkuk 1:1; Habakkuk 2:2-3)**.

- Habakkuk knew what to look for or how to seek and discern the voice of God **(Habakkuk 2:1)**.

- Habakkuk feared the Lord **(Habakkuk 3:2)**.

- Habakkuk takes his seat of authority in prayer – exhorting God, releasing God's will and remembering what God has already done **(Habakkuk 3)**.

There are so many different and distinct nuggets of revelation that we can draw from these truths. But the one we must focus on is this: "Habakkuk's submission to God as a prophet and watchman gave him access to and authority in the scribal realm of dreams and visions. It also gave him POWER to fulfill and propel his assignment of writing and publishing the oracles."

Dr. Kluane Spake, whom I deeply love and respect, wrote this in her exceptional book, *Apostolic Authority*: "Seems like everyone wants the power of God – the problem is that first we need to apprehend His authority."[16]

She clarifies that the word power is correctly translated as *dunamis* in Greek. It is from this translation that we get the word "power" not authority. Dr. Spake states: "Dunamis power belongs ONLY to God. (Humans don't possess *dunamis* power – but they can use His power within

---

16 Kluane Spake, "Apostolic Authority," (2007: Atlanta), p. 33.

33

His limits.) Dunamis is energetic power, explosive power or a demonstrative power that can reproduce itself. It is a demonstration of God's force.[17] Exousia is the mistranslated word. Exousia signifies the authority and liberty to operate and govern in God's power and anointing. The Bible continually talks about authority but we miss it. Jesus is the (exousia) authority of God (1 Cor. 1:24). The Gospel is the exousia of God (Rom. 1:16). True AUTHORITY is DELEGATED POWER. **The more of His authority we have, the more of God's power is released and revealed through us.** We do not need more power; we need God's authority to move in His power."[18]

Habakkuk walked in God's authority. We have God's authority. Dr. Spake taught me that exercising authority has little to do with simply *being* in charge. After all, there are many people in charge of things that have absolutely NO authority and are completely powerless. I have learned that while everyone has indeed received a measure of authority from God, they must grow and develop in that authority; and stand as wise stewards in the midst of it. Listen, there is so much in this discussion that I cannot BEGIN to develop it in its fullness for you here. I recommend the book, *Apostolic Authority* by Dr. Kluane Spake. It is perhaps, the most comprehensive book I have ever encountered about apostles and apostolic authority. It is a must have for 21st Century **Ephesians 4:11** leaders.

Listen, Dr. Spake discusses how important it is to learn about one's own authority.[19] And this, scribes of the King, is what I am speaking of here – in this moment. Habakkuk recognized that God was in charge – period. He recognized that he could only move within the boundaries that the Lord had set for him. **So, he took the time to explore, identify and perfect his understanding of those boundaries.** He recognized that he was given God's authority to do certain things within his territory or sphere of

---

[17] Ibid, 33.
[18] Ibid, 35.
[19] Ibid, 47.

influence, and he learned to exercise that authority within his own specific measure. This gave him access to untold treasures – his spiritual storehouse - and revelation concerning his calling, assignment and purpose. Ultimately, it gave him the access needed to present the "hard question" to God.

You can explore and exercise your delegated authority in God – even in the realm of dreams and visions. Remember, Habakkuk BOLDLY approached his rampart. He determined in his heart that he would remain there until God answered. **He used his gift of SIGHT and ACCESS to the dream realm to retrieve the answer sought.** Most of us wait for revelation to drop from the sky! But scribes, Habakkuk teaches us that we DO NOT HAVE TO WAIT. We can retrieve revelation. We can seek it out – using the authority and access that we already have.

I hope this is becoming clear to you for the purpose of this teaching. Dr. Spake teaches that Christ ushered in an "incomprehensible **revolution** of authority."[20] She states that the resurrection of Christ "placed the authority of God (which had always been exhibited externally), into the hearts of every believer to use."[21] What does this mean to us? It means that we have an even greater level of authority than what was extended to Habakkuk! It means that every person has the opportunity to develop their authority to fulfill their calling and purpose.

Listen, we have extensive authority through the precious gift of Christ. Through my journey with the Lord, I also realize that this authority has unfolded hand-in-hand with my spiritual development and the growth of my relationship with God; the right understanding of the scripture; by revelation as I mature and most importantly – through continued acts of submission to the authority of Christ and obedience to His instructions. In other words, if we want to walk in authority we must learn to fully submit

---

[20] Ibid.
[21] Ibid.

to authority. This includes submitting to Christ and those he has placed in positions of command in relationship to us. **Dr. Spake describes it this way:** Primary authority belongs to those who have the initial right to command; and delegated authority is the right to command and to enforce obedience which was given to someone by the one holding primary authority.[22] Isn't this profound?

In *The Scribal Realm of Dreams and Visions,* we are reinforcing so many foundational areas of our faith. Among the most significant is that we grasp how important it is to show Christ we love Him by being obedient students. We are being reminded that every single step in the process is important. We are seeing that NOTHING and I mean absolutely NOTHING God commands us to do is wasted.

---

[22] Ibid.

Humanity: His Ultimate Oracle

For in him we live and move and exist. Indeed, as some of the poets among you have said, We are actually his children.
~ Acts 17:28

THE ORACLE

We are going to take a closer look at what is meant by the term "oracle." Depending on the translation of the bible you choose, oracle has been used interchangeably with the terms prophecy and burden. Most scholars agree that while "prophecy" is, in a sense, what an oracle represents... it has a more *specific* meaning and use than what the word prophecy is able to convey. Some scholars insist that the term "oracle" is mistranslation in English bibles and the term means "burden of the Lord" – specifically as it relates to what is of grave concern to God himself at any particular time or dispensation. It literally means *to carry* as in a heavy load or weight.

Clarifying this is necessary as we continue to dig into the scribal realm of dreams and visions. A clear definition will assist us in gaining insight relating to how we should "view and observe" the oracles Habakkuk received from God. Take a look at how the Holman's Bible Dictionary defines the term:

> "The term oracle refers both to divine responses to a question asked of God and to pronouncements made by God without His being asked. In one sense, oracles were prophecies since they often referred to the future; but oracles sometimes dealt with decisions to be made in the present. Usually, in the Bible the communication was from Yahweh, the God of Israel. In times of idol worship, however, Israelites did seek a word or pronouncement from false gods **(Hosea 4:12)**. Many of Israel's neighbors sought oracles from their gods. Although the word oracle is not very frequent in the Old Testament, oracles were common in that period. This difference occurs because the Hebrew words translated 'oracle' may also be translated as 'burden,' 'saying,'

'word,' etc. Translations are not consistent in how they render these Hebrew words."[23]

Interestingly, the 1828 Webster's Dictionary of the English Language supports the use of the word oracle noting that scripture signifies it as the communications, revelations or messages delivered by God to prophets.[24] Contemporary dictionaries, commentaries and encyclopedias indicate that both terms share some truth in that "oracle or burden" is understood to mean the "Word of the Lord" or "Word of God." **It indicates that a Word has come directly from God himself as a directive, a clear instruction.** Habakkuk's oracles truly fit this explanation. It is through this view that the Holy Bible is often referred to as a *living* oracle and equated with the power to *quicken*.[25] The Holy Bible is viewed corporately as a cohesive document released directly from God.

Hebrews 4:12 NIV states: *"For* **the Word of God** *is* **alive and active.** *Sharper than any double-edged sword,* **it penetrates even to dividing soul and spirit, joints and marrow;** *it judges the thoughts and attitudes of the heart."*

For the purpose of our discussion, it is fair to say that the term oracle and burden are interchangeable but with the understanding that its use refers specifically to Words released by God in response to "a question asked of Him and to pronouncements made by God without being asked." By pronouncements, we are speaking of declarations, decrees, assertions, judgments and statements that are ***non-negotiable and final.*** We accept the

---

[23] StudyLight.org, Holman Bible Dictionary Online: Oracles, http://www.studylight.org/dictionaries/hbd/view.cgi?n=4726

[24] Webster's American Dictionary of the English Language, Oracle, Published in 1828 (Public Domain), https://ia601406.us.archive.org/16/items/americandictiona01websrich/americandictiona01websrich_bw.pdf

[25] King James Bible Verse, Definition of the word Oracle, http://www.kingjamesbibleverse.com/definitions/o/oracle/

term "oracle" as meaning the "Word of the Lord." Habakkuk's oracle or burden distinctly fits this description; and stands apart from present prophetic ministry or general prophecy as it relates to releasing words of encouragement, comfort and exhortation. General prophecy is a huge and extremely significant part of the scribal realm of dreams and visions. But our understanding of an oracle... helps us get a better handle on everything that the dream realm releases.

Some of you who are reading this book right now will receive oracles that will answer specific questions or provide direct answers for the population of people you serve. There is a need for us to be able to discern the difference and recognize the weight.

THE ORACLE WITHIN THE ORACLE

John 1:1-5, 14 NIV says, *"In the beginning **was the Word,** and **the Word** was with God, **and the Word was God. He was with God in the beginning.** **Through him all things were made;** without him nothing was made that has been made. **In him was life, and that life was the light of all mankind.** The light shines in the darkness, and the darkness has not overcome it."*

*"**The Word became flesh and made his dwelling among us.** We have seen his glory, the glory of the one and only Son, who came from the Father, full of grace and truth."*

This passage recaps some foundational truths of our faith:

- The **Word of God** existed from the beginning.
- The **Word** was with God.
- The **Word was God**, the oracle.
- God made all things.
- God is the source of all things that were made.
- All things that were made by God are His **Word**.

- **All life, including mankind, came from God.**
- Life is in God.
- Life is the **Word**.
- Life is in the **Word**.
- Life is light.
- This light is the **Word**.
- Light was shining in darkness.
- Darkness could not overtake light.
- We are the light called human kind, his image.
- Darkness cannot overcome humankind.
- We see God's glory in the **Word**.
- Darkness cannot overcome light.
- Darkness is not more powerful than light.
- Light always shines in darkness.
- **The Word** was and is Christ.
- Christ became **The Word** made flesh.
- The **Word** lived among us in the flesh.
- The **Word** still lives, dwells among us.
- Christ carried God's glory.
- God's glory is in **His Word**.
- Christ is God's glory.
- God's glory is **the Word.**
- God is also the glory.
- Christ is full of grace and truth.
- **The Word** is full of grace and truth.
- We are in Christ.
- We are in **the Word.**
- We are the **Word** made flesh.
- We see God's glory in the **Word**.
- We carry God's Glory.

I want you to see that not only does God release oracles, but **HE IS** the oracle. He is the source of every oracle. Let us take a look at **John 1** again, but this time… we will view it prophetically with the underlined words replaced with the term ORACLE.

John 1:1-5, 14 NIV says, *"In the beginning* __*was the ORACLE,*__ *and* __*the ORACLE*__ *was with God,* __*and the ORACLE was God.*__ __*THE ORACLE was with God*__ __*in the beginning.*__ __*Through THE ORACLE*__ *all things were made; without* __*THE ORACLE*__ *nothing was made that has been made.* __*In THE ORACLE WAS LIFE, and*__ __*that life WAS the ORACLE of ALL MANKIND.*__ *The* __*ORACLE*__ *shines in the darkness, and the darkness has not overcome it."*

__*"The ORACLE*__ __*became flesh*__ __*and made his dwelling among us.*__ *We have seen* __*THE ORACLE'S*__ *glory, the glory of the one and only Son, who came from the Father, full of grace and truth."*

Can you comprehend it? **Try it with the interchangeable term "burden."** It will bless you… and cause you to see that the Word of the Lord is our most treasured possession in the heaven and earth. (Religion will go haywire here… and reject what God wants to reveal.) This view of "oracle and burden" blesses me, especially when I consider the ANSWER Habakkuk saw…. that explained why God allowed bad things to happen to His chosen people.

The ultimate Word of the Lord – the ultimate pronouncement IS GOD and it is the fulfillment of all that He accomplished, finished. We were, have and are hidden in **THE ORACLE**. We were and are a part of the first pronouncement or oracle God ever released out of His mouth at creation: *"Let there be light!"* Remember, **John 1:1-5** tells us that the *"life* of **the oracle** was the *light* of all mankind."* This is another way of stating that our existence – every soul that has ever lived - is the result of the "Word of God or the Word of the Lord" released into the earth.

God's servant David recognized this as it related to his own life. In **Psalm 40:7-8** NIV he declared: *"Then I said, Here I am, I have come— it is written about me in the scroll. I desire to do your will, my God; your law is within my heart."* In **Isaiah 11** the Word of the Lord came that prophesied the lineage of Christ through David's father Jesse. David recognized the oracle that was written concerning Him.

Let this sink deeply into your hearts.

While we may not be able to find our names and our specific story in Torah and the Prophets, *rest assured* that our scroll, your scroll is written in Heaven! When we really and I mean really grasp the weight of this, we will NEVER knowingly discard the "mysteries and secrets" hidden in our own dreams and visions because we will make the connection, the true connection of its possible weightiness before God.

Jeremiah 31:30-33 CJB, *"Here, the days are coming," says ADONAI, when I will make a new covenant with the house of Isra'el and with the house of Y'hudah.*

*"It will not be like the covenant I made with their fathers on the day I took them by their hand and brought them out of the land of Egypt; because they, for their part, violated my covenant, even though I, for my part, was a husband to them, says ADONAI. For this is the covenant I will make with the house of Isra'el after those days, says ADONAI: **I will put my Torah (ORACLE) within them** and **write it on their hearts;** I will be their God, and they will be my people. No longer will any of them teach his fellow community member or his brother, 'Know ADONAI'; **for all will know me, from the least of them to the greatest;** because I will forgive their wickednesses and remember their sins no more."*

Now, consider this. The Apostle Paul uses this analogy in **2 Corinthians 3:2-3** CJB in his letter to the Corinthian church: *"You yourselves are our*

44

letter of recommendation, written on our hearts, known and read by everyone. **You make it clear that _you are a letter from the Messiah (ORACLE)_ placed in our care, _written_ not with ink but _by the Spirit of the living God,_ not on stone tablets but on human hearts.** *"*

We are "oracles" within "the oracle"…whom God calls to release oracles. We are writing what was written. We are the continuation of ancient prophecies and revelation sealed, locked in ancient scrolls. Whether our lives prophesy life or death – it is still the Word speaking. As sons, we are walking out the declaration of doing greater works. We are still experiencing the effects of the outpouring on the Day of Pentecost. We are still receiving oracles through dreams and visions… that await their appointed times.

Christ said this in **John 16:12-13**, *"I have much more to say to you, more than you can now bear.* **But when he, the Spirit of truth comes,** *he will guide you into all the truth. He will not speak on his own;* **he will speak only what he hears, and he will tell you what is yet to come.** *He will glorify me because **it is from me** that **he will receive what he will make known to you.**"*

THE WORD (CHRIST) – **THE ORACLE** – GUIDES HOLY SPIRIT IN THE EARTH in our PRESENT DAY.

HE DWELLS WITH US

And I heard a great voice out of heaven saying, Behold, the tabernacle of God is with men, and he will dwell with them, and they shall be his people, and God himself shall be with them, and be their God.

~ Revelation 21:3

UNDERSTANDING THE
SCRIBAL REALM

Now, let's get a good grip on understanding the scribal realm. My earliest memory of being fascinated with writing goes all the way back to 1977. I was six years old and my first grade teacher was reading a poem in celebration of Black History Month entitled, *"The Negro Speaks of Rivers,"* by Langston Hughes. I cannot explain it, but I still remember what each poetic line sounded like as she artistically enunciated each word as if it were her own. I sat in my tattered wooden desk in awe, hanging on every word as she recited the poem and explained its significance in a way that first graders, like myself, could understand. She loved talking to us about the beauty of being Black and the treasures hidden in my heritage. Although I was young, the scribe in me was ignited and a deep, passionate love for poetry, reading and rhetoric was born. My imagination was so hyped that I can remember dreaming of reciting poetry to thousands, and giving speeches to any group willing to listen. Even then I was standing in the scribal realm.

I can't remember a time in my life from that point forward that I was not without pen, paper, a speech, a song and a poetic flow. The kids would stand around during recess and listen to me flow with poetry, read short stories or sing. I can remember one friend in particular calling everyone on the playground: "Y'all come on! Resa fixin'-to sing!" Others would sometimes join in. Yes, we did that in grade school…in addition to telling those "yo-mama" jokes we loved so much. Whatever God had placed in me scribally, though unknown to me at the time was being revealed in childhood.

Pen and paper were my best friends – not people. It's where I shared my fears, hopes and dreams; and the place where every child's secret found a safe place. It was also on paper that I would come to encounter God some twenty-two years later. Writing to me, even now, is as essential as breathing. It is how I view and see life. I know some who are reading this can identify. Looking back, it is evident that Holy Spirit had been wooing me scribally my entire life and I didn't even know it. I was always drawn to anything writing-reading related, and ultimately embarked upon a career in journalism after graduating from college and won several awards as a print news reporter. I went on to write for magazines, hold positions as a news editor, work in grants, fundraising and even as a communications director for several nonprofit, educational and governmental organizations. Every bit of this activity was representative of the work of a scribe.

Even more amazing was that I never made a career choice that I did not enjoy. But the very moment I surrendered to Christ, the heavenly or revelatory realm of the scribe fell upon me at a massive level. I began to experience those Holy Spirit awakenings in the night season. And for nearly four years, as I mentioned in the introduction to this book, I simply couldn't stop writing and releasing what was being poured into my spirit. I was in a Holy Spirit initiated scribe school, completely unaware.

THE WORD "SCRIBAL"

We have been using the word *scribal* often. It literally refers to the processes and/or activities surrounding anything and everything that a scribe does. Merriam-Webster's Online Dictionary simply defines it as any activity "relating to or due to a scribe."[26] It can't get any simpler than that.

Writing happens to be my first love as it relates to my calling. It is important that every prophetic scribe understands that writing is only *one aspect* of scribal activity. Scribal ministry, however, encompasses a broad range of functions – everything from letter writing and book publishing to event planning, finance, contracts and grants. In scripture, the most visible

---

[26] Meriam Webster Online, http://www.merriam-webster.com/dictionary/scribal

scribes were responsible for copying, protecting, preserving and publishing Torah. They were also in charge of numerous administrative functions to support the congregation and/or the work of the kingdom in governmental and community facets.

Scribes we descend from Moses original leadership team in **Numbers 11**. Remember, the Great Council that was originally formed consisted of 70 members – equally divided into elders, chief priests and scribes, with Moses as the High Priest. This was the first government God set up for the Nation of Israel. The leaders, which included holy scribes, were (1) handpicked from known leaders; (2) sent on a consecration; (3) received an outpouring similar to Acts 2; (4) were ordained and sent in a public ceremony; (5) prophesied in the camp with Moses; and (6) were given governmental authority in the kingdom to enact laws, serve as justices and put all the policies and procedures in place necessary to run the Kingdom. Were some of those scribes also writers? Recorders? Of course they were.

So you see, The Scribal Anointing® is not just about writing and publishing books --- but also about "administrating and governing" at an apostolic level. The first scribes were placed in AUTHORITY and ruled in their delegated capacity with Moses. Some of the top accountants, bookkeepers, negotiators and entrepreneurs in the Kingdom... began their biblical journey as scribes. They were skilled and anointed men with expertise in judicial matters, record keeping, research, program development, note taking or recording, genealogy, planning, finances, clerical duties, judicial responsibilities, structuring government, planning and directing feasts, creating processes, handling legal matters, settling disputes, etc. There are absolutely too many roles or scribal functions to list in this book. Even more taxing are the roles and responsibilities that can be expounded upon from just one area among those mentioned. Can you see the depth of the scribal activity that may have been in the midst of Moses? Can you see how these roles may have played out in both Old and New Covenants and can be seen today? Scribal ministry went through some major transitions over that period of time. However, their wide-range of functions remained.

When we speak of scribal functions today, most people think writing only; and are primarily familiar with the role of copyists, teachers and interpreters of the Law. But scribal ministry as a whole is being clarified. With this broadened perspective from **Numbers 11** and **Matthew 13:52**, we can now identify a *prophetic* scribe as a scribe who fulfills his or her scribal calling solely under the instruction, guidance and anointing of Holy Spirit. What makes a scribe prophetic is not the gift itself; but the recognition or calling to administrate the scribal function from that instructed place. It is truly a "not my will but your will be done" calling.

Was I a scribe in my early life? Yes. All the signs were there. I was not prophetic, but I was a scribe. My strongest anointing was primarily in writing, but I also had clues that pointed to administration and instruction as well. These were things that I was being developed in and that would grow up with me that I would not recognize until much later in life. Truly, the gifts and callings of God are irrevocable.

There are also scribes operating in the earth today who did not sense the calling of a scribe or begin walking out the "signs of a scribe" until much later in their spiritual growth and maturation process. This is also not unusual. These scribes were "suddenly awakened" – plucked out of where they were and literally plopped right in the middle of scribal ministry. I call them "sleepers," God's secret operatives whose activation is directly tied to a specific, appointed time in Heaven and earth. They cannot enter *the scribal realm* – until it is their time of awakening and sending. And when they do, everything they need to administrate that calling is placed before them.

Many of these scribes are just as must "called scribes" as those who were active from the womb. God simply had an appointed time for them to experience their calling.

DEFINING THE SCRIBAL REALM

Now that we have brought clarity to what it means to be scribal, let us gain insight into the word *realm* as we reference it here. Biblically, the word describes a spiritual and/or natural territory, domain or kingdom in which someone has sovereign authority or rule. We already know that God has sovereign authority over everything. We also know that Habakkuk had governance over Judah as a prophet and watchman. While *realm* is a common term, it is not one that is used widely in scripture. The following references place its limited biblical use in context.

Ezra 7:23 KJV says, *"Whatever is ordered by the God of heaven is to be performed exactly for the house of the God of heaven; for why should wrath come against the __REALM of the KING and his SONS?__"*

Daniel 6:3 AMP says, *"Then this Daniel, because of the extraordinary spirit within him, began distinguishing himself among the commissioners and the satraps, and __the KING planned to appoint him over the entire REALM__."*

John 6:62 AMP says, *"What then [will you think] if you see __the Son of Man ascending to [the REALM]__ where He was before?"*

These passages accurately clarify its meaning. We can now define the *scribal realm* as both a natural and supernatural territory, kingdom or domain in which there is a saturation of scribal activity, scribal functions of all kinds and scribal focus on a consistent, continuous basis. I firmly believe that specific "realms" exist for certain types of callings and anointings to be nurtured, developed or accessed for expansion and

53

distribution for God's unique purposes. In assessing my own scribal ministry, I also know that I am considered a "master" or someone who has been placed in a position of command in the "scribal realm" to affirm and guide others in the midst of their scribal ministries.

At this point, you should be understanding how all the things we have discussed up to this point fit or are coming together. In one sense, a scribal realm is a physical place. For example, a brick and mortar publishing company is overseen by scribes, saturated in scribal activity and immersed in a scribal atmosphere. A scribe who is passionate about this atmosphere could be considered as living in "a scribal realm." Whether the scribes are believers or not, their calling and purpose is revealed in their scribal environment. A grant writing seminar led by passionate and enthusiastic leaders is also an example of a type of scribal realm in the natural in which those who may love the craft gather to learn about new laws governing state, federal or foundation grants; and perhaps, learn to write them.

In another sense, the scribal realm can be a physical place AND a spiritual place. The spiritual place, however, is forever expanding because it is a state of being, a place of revelation, a place of prophetic and apostolic ministry... and it extends into the dimension of dreams and visions. It has an unlimited sphere of existence. In the very moment that I am typing this sentence in this specific book, I am in an expanding scribal realm in the spirit.

Finally, I want to make this one statement before moving deeper into this: While we have our individual scribal realm, we SHARE the scribal realm as a community. In other words, all prophetic scribes – though uniquely different – exist in corporate scribal family or scribal company; as well as in the scribal realm. Their lives are literally shaped by their scribal interests. **1 Corinthians 12** really expresses my thoughts here very well. Just as each scribal family or scribal company had its area of expertise, influence and mastery in the scriptures... we still exist this way today! Yet, we are one corporate body with a heart cry for the ultimate goal – reconciliation.

In the early part of my ministry, I spent an enormous amount of time nurturing an evangelist poetry group right here in Greater Atlanta. My connections, influence and authority during that time period was pretty much centered on the local church, community coffee houses and events we either hosted or participated in with others. While we were very effective in our mission in that season, our "scribal realm" in the natural was limited, our boundaries defined. Over time, God expanded that realm. We transitioned from evangelistic ministry to apostolic ministry and our scribal realm is global at this point – but still very specific to the population of people and the assignment that must be walked out. This is yet another way that we can view the scribal realm as a physical territory or a specific sphere of influence.

For several years, my writing was primarily testimonial. So the atmosphere that was created generally dealt with healing, deliverance, personal breakthrough, etc. As I became "the healed," the realm shifted! I found myself operating in a greater capacity as a watchman and a prophet within my assigned area. In this sense, you can also see how the scribal realm can be "that specific." Some scribes operate in a "financial realm" – where they are able to access insight into financial prosperity, stewardship, accountability, and all areas of wealth. Other scribes may operate in an aspect of the realm of recording – where they are able to tap into new technologies to that will propel the Gospel. Scribal prophets, whose ministries are set over specific territories, might enter realms in which they receive oracles – like Habakkuk – specifically for the people to whom God has given them charge over. So as you can see, there are numerous types of realms available to strengthen, sharpen or otherwise propel the calling of a scribe.

YOUR SCRIBAL REALM OF DREAMS & VISIONS

I was fascinated with fairytales as a young girl. I loved playing princess, dressing up and pretending along with my favorite Disney characters. Whenever someone spoke of *realms*, I would light up! I immediately thought of exclusive magical, majestic kingdoms that were located in secret, hard to find places. You know, places you had to "tap the heels of your shoes" to get to. I dreamed of fairies, flying and fairy god-mothers. The movies Wizard of Oz, Cinderella, Peter Pan, Beauty & the Beast and Snow White come to mind as I type this. Yes, I know this might not be a religious analogy; but it pretty much captures the "mystery and child-like innocence" often associated with realms. There is an agreement among people which supports the premise that the impossible happens in supernatural places just like this.

While we do not have any association whatsoever with sorcery or the work of magicians as believers, our spiritual lives are indeed walked out in a place of awe, enchantment and *child-like wonder* in the realm of the Spirit – *especially* as it relates to dreams and visions. Our entire biblical text is about the realm of God – His universe. And for some of us, our dream realm is just as mystical, if not more so, than any kingdom a Disney or Warner Brothers film could ever bring forth.

God taught me early in my journey that the dream realm was another aspect or part of learning to walk in the Spirit *and* live by the Spirit. **Galatians 5** defines what walking in the spirit looks like and how abandoning our old nature is necessary if we plan to live and dwell as sons of God. The Apostle Paul says this in **verses 16-17** NIV: *"What I am saying is this: **Run (route, order, construct) your lives by the Spirit.** Then you will not do what your old nature wants. For the old nature wants what is contrary to the Spirit, and **the Spirit wants what is contrary to the old nature.**"*

Part of this "running your lives by the Spirit" for the prophetic scribe truly involves embracing the supernatural realm of dreams and visions – especially if this is a key part of your listening, hearing and seeing. Not only are we to pursue the new man through submitting to Gods will, prayer, fasting, reading the word, learning obedience and all the other avenues we know well; but we are also supposed to open our hearts and minds to the many ways God desires to speak with us. Listen, the dream realm is truly one of the paths the Lord uses to teach us how to live in the Spirit.

Job 33:14-18 NIV says, *"For God does speak—now one way, now another— though no one perceives it. In a dream, in a vision of the night, when deep sleep falls on people as they slumber in their beds, he may speak in their ears and terrify them with warnings, **to turn them from wrongdoing and keep them from pride, to preserve them from the pit, their lives from perishing by the sword."***

Examine this passage closely to see what is promised to us personally through our dream lives.

We learn that God:

- Speaks to us in multiple ways for the purpose of getting our attention.

- Speaks directly into our ears as we sleep;

- Places the fear of the Lord in us;

- Warns us;

- Turns us away from sin;

- Turns us away from pride and toward humility;

- Protects us from judgment;

- Downloads revelation to us as we sleep;

- Keeps our lives from perishing; and

- Saves us from death, hell and the grave (spiritually and naturally).

What believer do you know who would not want this kind of saving grace? The first aspect of truly receiving our dream realm is accepting the fact that it is there to build us up as sons first! It is an incubator of instruction, guidance, chastisement, correction, realignment and love. We should desire this as much as we desire to receive other mysteries and secrets of the Kingdom. In fact, the greatest mystery we could ever endeavor to unfold is the one surrounding the significance of our *own* sonship.

Get to know who you are as a scribe in the realm of dreams and visions! Holy Spirit is in you to facilitate this area of learning.

If you are dreamer, you should always be in a place of surrender in the realm that God has designed for you. If you have rejected this part of your scribal journey, I want to encourage you to repent and embrace it right now… in this exact moment.

In my own life, God used the dream realm significantly to heal me. Like many of God's people, I was really messed up when I entered the Kingdom. For years, I had enjoyed the ungodly supernatural realm. I wasn't a dreamer… but I was already deeply involved in the occult. I was drawn to witches, warlocks, vampires and magic through movies, reading materials, video games, comic books, music, novels, etc. I spent hours lost in Dungeons & Dragons as a teen; and preferred video games that focused on magical realms, fantasy and extensive role playing. I consulted mediums, played Ouija boards, lead séances and a whole lot of other stuff. I lived on the dark side primarily out of curiosity. I wasn't knowingly or deliberately taking a stand against God. I was literally looking for a way to gain power over my own mess of a life. I just did not know Him... and was looking for anything that could help me navigate. On top of this, I was full of anger, unforgiveness, self-hatred, bitterness and the list goes on. My interests in the occult fed this. I loved hard core rap music and idolized some of the most notorious and violent rappers of the 90s. And my dream realm became a place a great deal of these things were dismantled, and nearly every dream in the night resulted in healing intertwined with a lament, a prayer or a poem that would stand as a testimony of my freedom and a tool to free others.

When we do not know who we are or whose we are, we will fall for every seducing force that presents itself to us... unaware. My life is an excellent example of this. I strongly believe that when the congregation begins to unapologetically move in the supernatural on multiple levels, including dreams and visions, we will see a record breaking harvest and biblically sound realignment. **Supernatural people require solid, supernatural understanding of the scriptures!**

The scribal realm will ALWAYS contain healing waters, wells of reconciliation and the unveiling of many mysteries.

THE DREAM REALM

We already know that the bare-bones definition of a dream is to have a vision while sleeping. I see every dream <u>God-gives</u> as a divine encounter with him in which we are receiving insight into His will and purpose regardless of the dream content. If we truly view Him as the dream giver, this perspective makes perfect sense. A vision is viewed as dream that takes place when a person is wide-eyed and awake.

The dream realm is a supernatural territory, domain or kingdom that exists in the spirit as a vehicle by which God sets up encounters with His sons. All people, according to **Acts 2**, have access to the realm of dreams and visions without exception. This, however, is no guarantee that a person will dream often; but it is a promise that at some point, they will have a dream encounter with God.

What makes the dream realm a "SCRIBAL" realm is simple: When a person dreams or have a vision, there will always be that overwhelming command to write, record or demonstrate what they have experienced, heard or seen. There will be a consistent atmosphere or environment in which some sort of scribal activity is *constantly, consistently* taking place.

For the most part, we have some pretty good ideas surrounding what writing and recording look like. Demonstration, on the other hand, is different. The prophet Ezekiel is an excellent example of a scribe who entered the scribal realm to meet God and then came out with instructions to "demonstrate" what he saw and heard in the style of perhaps, an actor or actress. He did everything from draw pictures on a brick to shave hair from his face. He brought a visual or demonstrative presentation of the prophecies he received from God to His people. (Take a look at the opening verses of **Ezekiel 4 & 5** for some excellent examples.)

Dreams Minister Barbie Breathitt describes God's use of the dream realm this way: "God uses dreams and visions to speak to us. **They bring the communications of heaven to earth.** God crafts each dream individually and uses them to speak to us in different ways and for different purposes. God reveals His plans and purposes through our dreams and visions. He shows us things ahead of time because *God wants to give us a clear vision to see beyond our present state.* He also creates dreams so we can see and hear the answers to our prayers. Dreams are a vehicle for bringing a peaceful resolve to the problem areas of life. Righteous people are given advance notice of the future through dreams and visions. This insures that they have plenty of time to prepare and align themselves for success and advancement."[27]

Breathitt's perspective is clear and on point in my opinion. We must also recall Habakkuk's experience. He entered the dream realm to receive an answer to a question presented to God. The dream realm is also a place of stern warning, protection, correction and direction **(Job 33:14-18).**

THE ATMOSPHERE OF THE SCRIBAL REALM

Within every supernatural realm of dreams and visions there is an atmosphere set for certain kinds of resources, awakenings, breakthroughs, transformations, establishments and/or releases. These atmospheres are as unique in the spirit realm as we are to one another as sons of God. Each atmosphere, as God has revealed it to me, is specific to our unique purposes in Heaven and earth. We literally enter the scribal realm of visions and dreams and retrieve the treasure that God intends to be released in us and/or in the earth.

When Jacob wrestled with the angel of the Lord, he exited that encounter with a completely new identity. When the apostle Peter descended from the open vision on Joppa his heart was forever changed concerning the will of God for gentiles. When Paul exited his encounter with God, he was no longer a persecutor of Christ, but a champion for Him. Each one of those dream realms – whether it was an open vision or a night vision – caused the dreamer to leave with something they did not previously have in their possession. They were NEVER the same in their hearts or in their mind. There will be a deposit made into your spiritual and natural man in the realm of dreams and visions whether we perceive its impact or not! Revelation doesn't always appear as a massive download, sometimes it

---

[27] CBN.com, Dream Interpretation According to the Bible, http://www1.cbn.com/700club/dream-interpretation-according-bible

grows with varying deposits... building for that ultimate moment of comprehension.

Generally speaking, an atmosphere is defined as the surrounding or pervading mood of the environment, the dominant mood or emotional tone that is set.[28] Atmospheres can be effective in releasing positive or negative change or outcomes depending on what is saturating them. In the scribal realm of dreams and visions, the atmosphere is saturated with pure ANOINTING – the yoke destroying and burden lifting power of God. When the anointing is present in the dream realm and the assignment is brought forth, you better believe that it will fulfill its "anointed" mission: Yokes will be destroyed. Burdens will be lifted. **The apostolic mandate to fulfill Isaiah 61 and ushering in the year of the Lord's favor will be made known.**

Remember, we are not talking about demonically influenced dreams here. We are talking about dreams and dream encounters inspired by God! Even if there are seemingly frightening things in dreams encountered by God, there will STILL BE an element or call to establish and or build according to **Isaiah 61**. God does nothing without his eternal purpose ALWAYS being at the center. There is absolutely no exception to this.

Habakkuk understood this. The scribal realm of dreams and visions consists of the scribal activity and atmosphere that defines who God has called that specific scribe to be. When I am in my scribal realm as a mature believer, I completely understand what is going on... and what is expected of me. In those early years, I did not understand WHY I was waking up in the middle of the night to write or record. But the more I obeyed God, the more I learned, understood.

---

[28] Dictionary.com, Definition: Atmosphere, http://dictionary.reference.com/browse/atmosphere

The atmosphere of the dream realm can help the scribe:

- Learn God's ways
- Heal and grow
- Find comfort
- Develop in all areas of prayer
- Build trust in God
- Identify his/her calling and purpose
- Avoid wrecking his/her ship
- Develop an identity in Christ
- Develop discernment
- Know and recognize the heart and mind of God
- Know and recognize the voice of the Lord
- Identify the burdens of the Lord
- Establish the plans and purposes of God
- Transform into a present day scribe
- Prophesy with clarity and accuracy
- Distinguish between oracles and prophecy
- Identify the plots and schemes of the adversary
- Learn to walk in the spirit
- Perfect mastery as a seer
- Perfect mastery as a scribe
- Perfect mastery as a watchman
- Perfect listening, hearing, seeing
- Access deeper realms of heaven
- Identify specific storehouses for certain treasures
- Access the treasures of the storehouse
- Access specific supernatural keys
- Guard hearts from false doctrines, false teachers
- Distinguish between soulish dreams & God dreams
- Develop a deeper hunger and thirst for God
- Develop a deeper love for God's Word
- Develop a heart of humility and brokenness

- Prepare to meet and receive from God supernaturally
- Learn to inquire of the Lord without fear
- Grow in boldness and courage
- Refine their relationship with God
- Grow in revelatory understanding
- Develop a solid prayer life
- Learn to lean on God's understanding, not their own
- Sharpen discernment
- Recognize critical scribal assignments
- Understand the timing of God
- Clearly identify the counsel of God
- Rightly divide the Word
- Avoid calamity, spiritual death, natural death
- Help my family members and loved ones
- Fine tune spiritual research skills
- Gain access to the scrolls, the archives of heaven's library
- Learn to communicate with angels
- Solicit input and insight from angels
- Publish the burdens of God in the earth
- Identify their specific realms of influence and authority
- Release scribal mantles in the earth
- Develop strategies, polices and protocols
- Establish scribal government
- Remain encouraged, hopeful and in faith
- Legislate and petition God through inquiries, intercession and prayer
- Learn to reason with God
- Grow in boldness
- Receive refining, perfecting and rest
- See future events
- Engage in personal deliverance
- Engage in corporate deliverance

- Receive affirmation and confirmation from God in my calling, purpose and destiny
- Navigate life with Holy Spirit
- Unlock the secrets and mysteries of God's Word
- Engage in and understand supernatural activity

Your dream realm will save your life! It's not just about bringing treasures out for someone else. It's primarily about BUILDING THE BELIEVER! As long as we believe the dream realm is unimportant, we will limit our access to our great spiritual treasure, heritage. *Earnestly, the people of God are limited ONLY by their level of belief.*

GOD'S TREASURE HUNTERS

In scripture, the word treasure is often synonymous with storehouse or repository. Both reference places where something of great merit and value is stored and protected. We also know that the storehouse is representative of *secret* treasures and mysteries laid aside for us by God. These treasures are not limited to wisdom only, but physical manifestations of knowledge, wisdom, healing, restoration, wealth and favor.

In this study, Father revealed Habakkuk to me as a treasure hunter. My understanding of this is simple: A treasure hunter is someone who deliberately searches "for a specific type" of treasure. Dedicated treasure hunters rarely look for just ANY KIND of treasure. They seek specific kinds. Don't forget this. We are not talking about digging your hand in the bottom of a bag hoping to pull something, anything that might be of value. A true treasure hunter knows *what* he is searching for and <u>WHERE TO GO TO FIND IT</u>. In addition, they have the right gear to search with and recognize the treasure when it is found.

In Habakkuk's realm of authority, he walked this understanding out. He deliberately positioned himself as a treasure hunter in search of the oracles of God. Had he not done so, the people of God would never have received understanding concerning their circumstances and we might not have such detailed treasure today. He was on a deep, uncommon, supernatural search of *treasure*. And guess what, the scribal realm of dreams and visions gives us access to the storehouse. Let's take a look at **Matthew 13:52** again. It reads:

*"Therefore every writer, secretary or recorder who has become a disciple to follow [God's] precepts and instructions concerning the heart and mind of God is like **a master of the house** or owner who **LEADS OUT or BRINGS FORTH** of his **KINGLY, REGAL STOREHOUSE** things uncommon, of a new kind or fresh and from an earlier time.*

As you know, this passage of scripture is THE foundation for understanding present day scribal ministry. While it is indeed a parable concerning who we are as scribes, it is also a point of profound "transition" for "scribes of the old regime" to "present day scribes under the order of Christ."

Remember, up until Christ's ministry began – only scribes were tasked with interpreting the scriptures! Christ interrupted and demolished that order with this PROFOUND statement in **Matthew 13:52**. When he was speaking to His disciples here, He was basically telling them that they are equipped to interpret and teach the scriptures as the "scribes taught it"…but with access to a supernatural storehouse of revelation!

That storehouse spoken of in this passage of scripture is one that is accessible to scribes *instructed* in the *Kingdom of Heaven*. It is an innate part of "the scribal realm." It is one more avenue God has given us to access treasures in heaven that are to be released in the earth, and in our earth. Habakkuk was able to search out and locate his storehouse in the dream realm released to him? How much more are we able to access with Holy Spirit in us?

We can be intentional in our desire to access this treasure!

The scribal realm of dreams and visions is an atmosphere and a realm created specifically for YOU by GOD to meet! Could this realm... be among the MANY rooms that Christ went to prepare for us in the house of God **(John 14:1-3)**? Could this be a place in eternity that we supernaturally abide? Could this be among the reasons that HOLY SPIRIT had to come? Could this be one of the ways Christ wanted to ensure that we could learn more about the Kingdom? After all he said, there were many other things He wanted to share with us but during his time on earth, his disciples were unable to bear them.

In this present season of the scribe, we have been charged with unlocking the secrets and mysteries of God's Word. We have learned from Habakkuk that we can position ourselves to seek what is in our storehouse – fresh, new and from ancient of days. We are indeed God's treasure hunters.

The dream realm has become a waiting room, a birthing room for my people, says the Lord. They sit and they wait for me to invite them to the banquet. They come by invitation and I meet them there with my treasure. In this season, I am limiting access to the waiting room – those places where they have found comfort. I am ushering them into the next level of their calling. I am raising up intentional dreamers. Those who will chase after specific divine encounters to answer specific questions that affect them personally, and affect my people.

I am causing them to place a demand on the dream realm according to their obedience. I am teaching them to pursue revelation, to pursue wisdom, to pursue knowledge, to pursue counsel, to pursue understanding by approaching me boldly in earnest, selfless inquiry. I am expanding the dream realm of my scribes, those who dream in and of words! I am teaching them to dig for treasure and access the storehouse I have prepared for them." Amen

RECOGNIZE YOUR SCRIBAL REALM

Scholars are blown away by Habakkuk's stellar writing style. Earlier, we established that he is often referred to in critical academic circles as a literary *genius*. And get this, Habakkuk was a poet. Not only did he write (as we have come to understand that meaning) the oracles God released to him in poetic form at the conclusion of the book, he engages in a profound, wild prayer of victory that captures the intensity of his renewed trust in God... and causes him to live up to the meaning of his name, "embrace or one who embraces."

There are no commands from God to write these exhortations of prayer; but a true prophetic scribe would long to put pen to paper anyway – even outside of God's command or urging. We are now witnessing – not only God's force in responding to this powerful prophet, but we are watching the prophet's faith increase and see his belief restored -- all resulting from an encounter in the scribal realm of dreams and visions.

Habakkuk 3:19 NIV says, *"The Sovereign LORD is my strength; he makes my feet like the feet of a deer, he enables me to tread on the heights."*

What a dramatic transformation! Now, let us take a closer look at the prophet's writing style.

David Henry Kyes said: "Habakkuk's command of language is excellent. Both his thought and expression are poetic. His style is the embodiment of boldness, sublimity and majesty. Here we find some of the finest parallelisms. It is impossible in translation to reproduce the abounding alliterations of the original or the prevailing poetic measure consisting of three principal words in a line."[29]

---

[29] David Henry Kyes, *The Literary Style of the Prophetic Books, of the English Bible*. (2013: London) Forgotten Books. (Original work published 1919)

Think about Kyes comments for moment.

Consider how the weighty oracles were in **Habakkuk 1 & 2.** You see, we might not normally consider the significance of this tidbit of information. What's even more prophetic is that very few people – outside of the life of the artist themselves - would connect an "oracle" as we now understand it to be, and much less a prophecy, with the release of creative expression. Even with the rise of prophetic poetic ministries over the past decade, and the growing understanding of scribal ministry – very few would legitimate prophetic poetry as prophecy. Habakkuk, however, proves a couple of things to us: (1) God made the connection; and (2) God loves creative expression. After all, we know through literary examination that most of Torah and the Prophets are written in poetry and prose.

As a poet, it is easy for me to fully embrace this aspect of Habakkuk's prophetic scribal ministry. Most of the poems that I write or have written, especially over the past decade, are direct streams of prophecy in poetic form. Habakkuk's experience, and that of other biblical prophets, prove that creative scribal ministry is not simply a form of prophetic release, but a preferred method of prophetic release by God. It also proves that the Lord MET SCRIBES in the "scribal realm of dreams and visions" specifically to give them messages to convey creatively and demonstratively using their academic skill. It forces us to consider whether Ezekiel and Jeremiah were really strange or if this was normal activity for the Kingdom of Heaven. It proves that God has no religious agenda or formula in releasing the Word of the Lord to His people – even critical, weighty messages like the one contained in **Habakkuk 2**. It also reveals to us that our Father enjoys being represented well – intelligently, with deliberate literary style.

We learn from Daniel that God values education.

Daniel 1:17 NIV, *"To these four men <u>God gave</u> knowledge and understanding of <u>all kinds of literature and learning</u>. And Daniel could* *understand visions and dreams of all kinds."*

Scribes of the King, this will surely send a number of religious heads rolling in the midst of our faith-based communities. God employed people to pursue formal education; and encouraged some of the most well-known prophets to learn in the schools of Babylon. But for you, it is of great benefit to know and recognize who you are. I pray that this intense discussion settles your questions surrounding WHY God might release a message to you in the style, format, tenor or tone the way He does. I pray that you find value in your education, training, skill and technique once submitted to Christ. We were meant to not only write and record; but do so with intelligence, SKILL and class. Remember, we are the fruit of an ancient order of scribes that continues in its God-tradition even until this very day.

For the "instructed scribe," this is the perfect place to throw down the mic and get free. The very nature of being instructed means that we must be "taught" not only of the Lord but in other areas if necessary. What was true for scribes of old still applies to scribes today. We've got to STOP allowing people to tell us how to present the Word of the Lord given to us.

The New Covenant consists of oratory genius and profound Greco-letter-writing techniques. Most of the New Covenant was written by Paul, and guess what: Scholars also commend him on the eloquence of his writing. The response of scholars to Habakkuk's writing style, however, indicates that he did not just write this book in poetic form... but that he was a passionate poet to his core! God didn't take that away from Him because He put that love for poetry in Him; and then used it for His glory. Poetic form also assisted with helping people remember. Those running with this vision, were running with poems that could be remembered!

Although Habakkuk's scribal realm was intense, it was a place where he saw WORDS and was able to transcribe those WORDS poetically. **What** is taking place in your scribal realm? What does your scribal realm look like? These are questions that every scribe who dreams must answer! Finally, do not walk away discouraged if you do not have formal training in writing or recording. This IS NOT about that. God uses us where we are in Him. However, those who have extensive skill must recognize that they are also called. In many religious circles, scholarship is despised. Scribes, find your scribal realm and embrace it.

PROPHETIC EXERCISE: YOUR SCRIBAL REALM

Right now, I want to challenge you to begin the process of identifying your scribal realm of dreams and visions. Outline at least four or five areas that you believe summarize the **kind or type of dreams and/or visions** you experience most frequently **that GOD directs you to write down, record or demonstrate**. If you are already recording your dreams and visions, this will be easier for you. You can open your dream journal, look at your most recent dreams of no more than three months in the past if possible and identify the main subject of those dreams.

Completing this exercise provides you with an opportunity to see what area God is targeting and/or highlighting in your life at present time. Then after you identify these areas, I want you to rate which type of dream or vision you have most frequently on a scale of 0 to 100 percent. I also want to suggest that you keep your answers brief, really brief.

Quick recap of the instructions:

- Review your dreams from the past three months.
- Outline the kind or type of dreams you are experiencing most frequently.
- Rate which kind or type of dream or vision you have most frequently on a scale of 0 to 100 percent.
- Keep your responses short.

Don't worry. I have provided an example of this activity below. My dreams over the past three months have fallen into the following categories (and I have been required by God to record them):

(1) **Dreams in the night about myself.** They relate to direction, warnings concerning direction, and overcoming fears associated with direction. Presently, I would say 25 percent of my dreams in the night fall in this category.

(2) **Dreams in the night about those in my inner circle in ministry.** I would say 20 percent of my dream realm rests in this category, and specifically addresses intercession, protection, positioning, healing and deliverance.

(3) **Visions in regard to personal prophecy to others.** I am in the midst of prophetic ministry often with my inner circle – sometimes daily. I prophesy out of the seer realm – recording what I see. I would say that 20 percent of my dream realm is through open visions.

(4) **I have open visions and dreams about the ministry of the scribe.** This book is an example of that. I would say 30 percent of my dream realm rests in this category in this season.

(5) **Dreams about world issues and world leaders.** I would say 5 percent of my dream realm rests in this category and is specific to the presidential election and countries in which I am traveling.

In this moment, these are the categories in which God is speaking to me the most in the scribal realm of dreams and visions. As you can see, my dream life is not that exciting compared to people who see world disasters, political intrigue, wars, famines and such. I do not mean this in a negative way. I am using it as a point of truth concerning how our dream lives can vary significantly from person to person, and from season to season for that matter.

Remember, our dream lives are always evolving. My specific dream pattern at the present time make perfect sense to me when I consider what is presently going on in my life. It is no surprise that I have found myself in this place "right now."

For example, this is some of what has taken place in my life during this time:

- I completely changed ministry assignments after 15 years of faithful service;

- I made some drastic and critical ministry alignments that were necessary for my future growth and accountability;

- I experienced some major relational changes within the leadership structure of the ministry entrusted me;

- I have received extreme spiritual pressure to publish several books relating to scribal ministry during this time period, of which this is the third one.

Listen, you can take this exercise further and look at "what is specifically" revealed in these dreams – peace, warfare, frustration, love, forgiveness, navigation, etc. Practicing this pattern every once in a while assists me with assessing what God might consider priority areas in my personal life. Quite frankly, we can become so busy, so distracted or otherwise preoccupied with the goings-on in our lives that we can't rightly evaluate where we are or where we need to focus. I believe what is taking place in our dreams can provide a broader view of what may be taking place in our lives.

In this hour, we cannot afford to get stuck at "dream interpretation." We have to realize that interpretations sometimes unfold over time. As a result, we must consider a broader or wider view surrounding the purpose of our dream experiences. The dream does not end or even begin with just dream interpretations! Some examples of what we might notice includes:

- **Repetition.** Am I receiving the same dream over and over.
- **Amplification.** Are certain parts of my dreams amplified above the rest?
- **Atmosphere Types.** Are certain atmospheres consistent in my dreams?
- **Emotion.** Are my dreams emotionally charged? If so, what are the dominant emotions.
- **Familiarity.** Are there familiar people in my dreams? Like common themes of families, ministers I know, etc.
- **Non-familiarity.** Do my dreams revolve around strangers, people I am unfamiliar with, people groups?
- **Heavenly Beings.** Am I engaging with angels?
- **God's Presence.** Am I in the direct presence of God, engaging with Him exclusively? Am I engulfed in the presence of Holy Spirit?
- **Personal Behavior.** What spiritual role do I play, if any, in my own dreams? Am I a deliverer, intercessor, recorder, prophet, preacher, etc.? What other role do I play?
- **Recording Activity.** Do you feel pressured or pulled to write or record my dreams or just some of them?

Often, our dream realm coincides with what is going on in our lives and ministries – even subconscious or repressed things. Scribes who are really bound and in need of deliverance, healing, etc. often have dreams that reveal God's heart for their breakthrough or healing. The process of recording can reveal this at extreme levels. I have noticed that when I am dealing with personal pain, disappointment or even a broken heart – my dream realm shifts for that time or season to a place of truth, comfort. When I am preparing for a major ministry assignment and God wants to reveal the heart and condition of the people to me... he does so in dreams by giving me scriptures, speaking topics that will bring forth His heart.

We can choose to record our dreams and make it a regular part of our spiritual discipline; but it is CRITICAL that we give special attention to those dreams we are "commanded or pressed" to record. Those dreams hold critical keys. Failing to record them can be detrimental to our progression and growth.

Now, look at the percentages you assigned to your present dream life. The highest percentage should represent an area where God is placing the most emphasis on in this particular time of your life. The lowest percentage should represent the area that is still a priority; but it ranks at the bottom of this list. Please know that this process is no sure fire guarantee of what God may be doing in you right now, but I believe it will be very useful to you... and critical in helping you organize your dream life and examine what is happening in it.

Finally, I want to encourage you to identify what type of writing or recording is being required of you. Then list the top three areas in their order of importance. For example, are you recording or writing:

(1) Actual dreams – line-by-line, generalizations
(2) Oracles and/or prophecy
(3) All kinds of prayers, declarations, decrees
(4) Poetry, spoken word, songs
(5) Business plans, marketing ideas, letters, lists, etc.
(6) Chapters of books, scripts, dialogue, etc.
(7) Character sketches, movie scenes, setting
(8) Sermons, bible studies
(9) Direction, strategy

(10) Witty ideas and sketches

(11) Other (List anything not mentioned here)

Based on what I have shared about my own dream life, I would choose the following in this specific order: 6, 1 and 9. Now, hold on to your self-assessment, we will need to review it again in the next section. Completing this exercise should help you see specifically how God may be meeting you in the midst of your relationship at time. I have found it very helpful and comforting at times.

Only God Knows

I know a man in Christ who fourteen years ago—whether in the body I do not know, or out of the body I do not know, [only] God knows—such a man was caught up to the third heaven. And I know that such a man—whether in the body or out of the body I do not know, [only] God knows—was caught up into Paradise and heard inexpressible words which man is not permitted to speak [words too sacred to tell].
~ 2 Corinthians 12:2-4 AMP

SCRIBES DREAM DIFFERENTLY

Dreams and visions can be extremely unique in *the scribal* realm. Our dream realm is conducive to and will ultimately center upon our calling. While the Father does deal with us personally in our dreams (and will continue to do so) many scribes will be positioned by Him to "download and receive" their scribal assignments, directions and vision almost entirely from visions and dreams. I am one of those types of prophetic scribes! This, people of God, is really what makes the scribal realm so UNIQUE to us! The scribal realm of dreams and visions really becomes our storehouse as discussed in **Matthew 13:52**. My prayer is that you will read through this chapter and become EMPOWERED, strengthened and affirmed as a scribal dreamer.

As you know by now, I love setting things up before we dig into fresh places of knowledge. So, I need to make these three statements – ensuring that we are on the same page:

(1) *There is no right or wrong way to dream or have visions.* This area is limitless and extremely subjective to the dreamer. No one person has all the revelation on dreams, visions, their interpretation or the process of interpretation. The only guarantee we have is that all *God-led dreams* will lead to the center of His heart, mind and will; and reflect what has already been written or demonstrated in His Word.

(2) *We cannot limit the dream realm to our own experiences or perceptions. Nor can we discount the experiences of other sons that we might not fully understand.* For scribes, these experiences can be wild and radical (remember Ezekiel). I am sure many people misunderstood Ezekiel's experiences and visions. As a result, we must learn to listen well, judge all things by foundations

in scripture, seek to discern at the hand of Holy Spirit and allow Holy Spirit to bring forth clarity in us.

(3) *No longer can we see ourselves as the odd-man-out.* You will find that many of your experiences are COMMON within the scribal community. We do not recognize them as common because many of us are not in the midst of "prophetic **scribal** groups." If you can connect with a "prophetic scribal" tribe, it will help you. Many prophetic people, while well intentioned, are unaware of this supernatural aspect of their lives in the scribal realm. In addition, affirmation concerning our experiences and encounters in the realm of dreams is non-existent; and there are limited places where a scribe can go to discuss their experiences and feel safe, unjudged. That odd-man-out syndrome ends today, in the name of Jesus! In this moment, you belong to a community that "gets you."

(4) *We dream differently.* In making this statement, please note that I am not declaring that we are "special" or set apart from any other believer. I am stating that THE WAY we dream is particular to the calling of a scribe that is upon our lives. Our dream realm creates an atmosphere that is conducive for "scribes" to fulfill the unique calling to write and record. We are employed in this capacity by the Lord himself! That's it.

Over the years, I have learned that our interactions within the scribal realm of dreams and visions differ from regular dreamers in five distinct areas. These areas can be described as: (1) Direct conversations; (2) Hearing words and sounds; (3) Engaging in a scribal prayer watch; (4) Mining for treasure; and (5) Dreaming with deep emotion. There are other areas, but these are the ones that I am compelled to share with you in this book. I have done my best to document all of these areas plainly in scripture, using examples that are fairly familiar.

DIRECT CONVERSATIONS WITH GOD & ANGELS

There are scribes who have walked the halls of our scribe school with this testimony: "God met me in my dream just like you are speaking to me right now. We had a complete conversation, and I woke up compelled to write what He said." In the same way, I have heard testimonies of similar accounts with angels. The key here is this: "God can convey the entire concepts of books, blogs, plays, skits, etc. in conversation with us. In fact, He can impart whatever He wills." These scribes were not only hearing words but engaging in dialogue with God and angels.

These conversations can be in the midst of open visions or in deep sleep. In Samuel's encounter with God in **1 Samuel 3:1-10** as a boy, he was in between both places – a vision and a dream. This in-between state is sometimes referred to as a waking dream. In the scribal experience, the conversation can result in the unfolding of complete oracles, prophetic words, chapters of books, elements of grants, business plan details or other scribal projects that were literally delivered to or unlocked in the scribe through the conversation. (Angel spoke to Zachariah, **Luke 1:5-23**; Angel met Joseph in a dream, **Matthew 1:20-21, 2:13**; Cornelius encountered an angel, **Acts 10:1-6;** an unknown scribe met with God in the high place and was commanded to write on the foreheads of men in a dream, **Ezekiel 9**.)

HEARING WORDS & SOUNDS

2 Kings 7:6 AMP, *"**For the Lord had made** the Syrian army **hear a noise of chariots and horses, the noise of a great army.** They had said to one another, The king of Israel has hired the Hittite and Egyptian kings to come upon us."*

Some prophetic scribes have dreams and visions in which they awaken with words, sounds or complete song compositions fully in their spirit. Often, there is no memory or recollection of an image driven encounter, but there remains a strong retention of complete discourse, song loops, music loops, key words, poetry, spoken word, prophesy, etc. In scripture, we know that the Lord has caused sound to rise through "non-visual" dream encounters like in the passage above. The Syrian army was not in a dream state… but what they heard was clearly akin to a vision. I know this may not seem like a vision at all, but listen – scribes really do dream differently. In a second this will make sense. Just bear with me.

For clarity, I am not speaking of hearing people talking around you "as you sleep" or having the noise from the television or digital device filter into your dream state. We are talking about people who clearly hear sound and words come forth from the realm of dreams and visions followed by an urgency to record what they hear. As the words and sounds come, the fully awake scribe is often immediately and actively engaged in the process of capturing what is being released in real time – whether composing music or rolling out poetic prophecy. It is common for some scribes to record as they hear instead of after they hear. When they record, it is uninterrupted until the last word is heard – and there is an inward release.

In sharing this, I want to clarify that prophetic scribes are fully aware of God's presence, the leading of Holy Spirit and the content to which they are writing when in a dream state. At no time are they separate from it as in a demonic experience in which someone else or something takes control of a person and writes on their behalf and/or without their knowledge – as in possession. In no way are we discussing anything associated with demonic possession or the demonic act of "automatic writing." Sometimes when sharing this type of information, we must be absolutely clear concerning the ways of Holy Spirit, the ways of God. We must remember that in everything we do under His guidance we are *willing* participants, serving as *co-laborers* in the Kingdom.

Daniel 7:11 speaks of hearing the SOUND of the horns *boasting*.

In another encounter, Daniel described what happened to him when he heard THE SOUND of God's words. **Daniel 10:9** NIV says: *"But I heard THE SOUND of HIS WORDS; and as soon as I HEARD THE SOUND of HIS WORDS, I fell into a deep sleep on my face with my face to the ground."*

In Daniel's encounter, he moved into a NON-VISUAL VISION… saturated with the SOUND of GOD'S words. I quickly realized that this prophet was experiencing: (1) the **weight** of the sound of the voice of the Lord; and (2) the **weight** upon the actual words spoken. The authority and power of God's word pulled him immediately into a kind of *trance*. In scripture, the word trance refers to "a spiritual state" in which you are taken from the natural realm by Holy Spirit into the dream realm. Remember, the SOUND of the voice of the Lord is like rolling thunder and the sound of rushing waters **(Exodus 19:19; Ezekiel 43:2; Psalm 29:3)**. His voice is described as having the capacity to divide flames of fire, shake the wilderness, cause calves to give birth, and strip forests bare when He speaks **(Psalm 29:9)**. I have come to understand that this is, perhaps, one of the reasons why the Lord may visit us in dreams in the night, speak to us by the Spirit in our inner man, and solicit the help of prophets and prophetic people to deliver His messages. Yes, I know God spoke directly to those he chose on many occasions. **But it is also possible that the sound of "his actual voice" alone may *sometimes* be too much to bear in our natural state.**

Let's not forget that there are many kinds of sounds that can be released in the dream realm – including sounds that have NEVER been heard before. We must also understand that like us, God can and does shift the tenor of His voice in scripture to convey His intended meaning.

Exodus 34:27 KJV, *"And the Lord said unto Moses, Write thou these words: for after the tenor of these words I have made a covenant with thee and with Israel."*

Those prophetic scribes who hear, really hear with great uniqueness and always under a command to write, record or demonstrate what they hear.

Scribal encounters may also involve the release of specific words – whether it is a single word, an actual phrase or a stream of words. The apostle John is a perfect example of this! Many times he was given the command to dictate words "he heard." **Revelation 3:14** NIV states, *"To the angel of the church in Laodicea* **write: These *are the words* *of the Amen,*** *the faithful and true witness, the ruler of God's creation."* Interestingly, the Apostle John's letters were addressed to the "angels" assigned to the churches. That's a powerful revelation here for another time. In the section, *The Scribal Storehouse: Treasure Hunting*, we will take an even deeper look at hearing words and sounds.

THE SCRIBAL PRAYER WATCH

Traditionally, the eight prayer watches are viewed from the perspective of a person waking up like clockwork at a designated time to pray. Let me tell you, my prayer life has never looked like this and for years, I thought I was missing God because of it. How could a minister not have a solid "prayer watch" in the midst of his or her life right? I began falling for the lie that perhaps I was not called to be minister. Instead of waking up in the night to pray for family, people, nations, presidents, etc., I was waking up writing and writing and writing some more. Don't get me wrong, I did wake up to pray every once in a while… but there was no consistency or prayer direction. The only thing consistent was the writing.

I can remember crying out to God asking him to give me a prayer watch, and give me a list of people and things to pray for in the night season. In my understanding at the time, God was ignoring me. Eventually, I shared "my struggle" with some intercessors whom I trusted. While they did not understand how to advise me, they did encourage me in my process to become a "prayer warrior" … an intercessor after God's heart. In addition,

I was praying… but I was doing so when I was led to, not on a schedule of any kind. I was discounting the fact that I did have a solid prayer life… even if it didn't follow a known pattern. And, my prayer life was spirit led not scripted.

At one point, I began setting my own alarm clock to get up and pray because I desperately wanted a prayer watch. I was going to show God that I could do this. Instead, I would wake up… lost, confused and end up writing anyway. I desperately wanted to be a part of this amazing movement that so many saints were experiencing. It never happened for me – at least not in this way.

Then, early one morning while writing to the Lord I heard this: "This has always been your prayer watch." I jumped up from the edge of my bed and literally threw my pen and paper to the floor. The tears began to flow from me like rivers as I entered this ugly cry. I looked down, and realized that for all of these years… many of my writings in the night season were cries to God for myself, family, friends, scribes… you name it. It just wasn't packaged in a way that I recognized. I realized that I had been standing on my rampart the entire time! Immediately, the Lord led me on a journey through the Psalms. Though I had read the Psalms many, many times – I had never read them like this. I quickly realized that David was a son who prayed and cried out often through his pen.

Scribes, there are three critical aspects to this that I want you to place deeply within your heart:

(1) The scribal prayer watch is legitimate. Instead of waking up like clockwork to get on my knees and pray – so to speak, I was waking up SCRIBING prayers, intercession, laments;

(2) Instead of praying directly, God may have you write out prayers, confess situations or circumstances, make declarations, decrees,

etc.; speak them into a recording device; or even shout out what you placed on paper; and

(3) God can use your scribal prayer watch as a place of birthing. I often refer to this as "writing into" a heavenly issue or circumstance. Some scribes write songs or sing through their prayer time. People of God, do not limit what God will do in these encounters in the Spirit. Just because others do not recognize or understand what you do or what God requires of you, it does not necessarily mean it is not God!

TREASURE HUNTING

As we walk through this, keep what we have covered concerning "hearing words and sounds" in your heart. I believe this section will build significantly upon it. As you can imagine, the scribal realm of dreams and visions is exploding with creativity; and saturated with revelatory insight concerning many projects prophetic scribes are destined to release in the earth. Secrets and mysteries concerning our kingdom assignments can be accessed here.

Just thinking about the unique treasure housed in our scribal realm brings me to **Deuteronomy 29:29** AMP, which reads: *"The secret things belong to the Lord our God,* ___*but the things which are revealed and disclosed belong to us and to our children forever,*___ *so that we may do all of the words of this law."* This passage stands out because it speaks into the critical connection between "revelation" and living out our roles as "sons." For our purposes, this scripture is reminding us that God reveals his secrets to us so that we can truly live as sons with Him. It speaks into our growth and maturation as well as our potential, purpose and destiny.

Sometime ago, I had the privilege of taking a trip to the Library of Heaven through my dreams. There are no words to really describe what I saw to the fullest. Under God's instruction, I connected with an illustrator who was able to capture a snapshot of it. I share that image with you below. Inside the library, I not only saw the volumes of books that were written concerning my own life, destiny and purpose and those of countless others; but I saw books that I had written and those that I am yet to write!

I saw angels standing as dedicated keepers over these living books/epistles and archives. (Living books are the books about us that we are still walking out.) And while I was near my area, an angel reached for a volume in the area where my life was stored...and opened it before me. In that same moment, the dream ended and I was tasked to write what I saw *and* understood from this encounter. In "the scribal realm" of dreams and visions, I believe we have been given special access to Heaven's library. I believe this library is a significant part of the "treasure" located in our unique, scribal storehouse mentioned in **Matthew 13:52**.

I have mentored scribes who have emerged from the dream realm with untold TREASURE --- character sketches, clothing designs for actors in their plays, visions for props and backdrops, opening scenes and conclusions, full chapters in novels or books of instruction, complete books, book titles, movie titles, movie scenes, backdrops, children's books and illustrations, cover designs, poetry and spoken word and very specific directives on how to implement certain aspects of the scribal vision entrusted to them. **I know these things are not coincidental.**

I produced a number of successful poetic plays early in my ministry, and the vision for all of them came from the scribal realm of dreams and visions. Perhaps the aspect of the scribal realm that has blessed me most over the years is hearing novelists say things like this: "I have been taken up by the Lord to hear the characters in my book speak and I have seen them interact. When I come out of that place, all I have to do is write what I heard and remember what I saw."

Not only did God give them the dialogue, but he also unveiled the character's personality! Isn't that amazing! Scribes have accessed scores for their plays and theatrical performances, heard background sounds for album projects, and emerged with colors and clothes for characters and so much more. Scribes, I believe our Father is that specific and intentional with us. God is calling us to BELIEVE in the supernatural realm again. He is calling us to TRUST our dream realm again. Scribes DREAM DIFFERENTLY!

SCRIBES, DREAMS & DEEP EMOTION

Of all the things we have discussed up to this point related to how scribes dream differently, this is perhaps one of the most critical areas. Religion and legalism won't relate well to what I am directed to share here. Nevertheless, it must be said.

Some prophetic scribes have had dream realm experiences saturated in emotion. They have experienced the weight of awe and joy, great fear – *the fear of the Lord* as well as the fear of death, the fear of man; and waves of deep, deep sadness, grief and loss that was conveyed through <u>God-inspired dreams</u>. I mention these specific emotions (although we are not limited to them in our discussion here) because for most dreamers, they often leave the greatest impression or mark upon us. I have learned that God can use the dream realm to impart a deeper compassion in us for his causes and purposes; or to allow us to receive a level of compassion for others. Emotion can also be catalysts for creating mood in plays, skits, music and song that will ultimately lead to a relational truth or point of awakening for the intended audience. Emotion can cause us to write, record or demonstrate an idea or concept that we would not be able to present otherwise.

When we speak of demonstration here, we are speaking of demonstrating by way of dramatic interpretation or presentation as in plays, skits, spoken word, acting, etc. from a holy place. We are also speaking of the gift of "describing emotion" in the midst of letters, novels, plays, etc. Remember, God also uses the dream realm to press us into the fear of the Lord and to warn of pending danger. How that looks is really specific to the encounter God desires to have with that specific dreamer.

Nebuchadnezzar said this in **Daniel 4:5** NIV: *"I saw a dream and **it made me FEARFUL**; and these fantasies as I lay on my bed and the visions in my head **kept alarming me**."* Note that God gave the king this dream, caused him to see his own judgement and through it placed the fear of the Lord upon him.

Despite what some of us may have been taught or have believed, EMOTIONS are not necessarily evil. **We were created to feel!** God gave us the *gift* of emotion. They enable us to cope with and enjoy life in our humanity and in our spiritual existence. They are also catalysts for experiencing the goodness of God and realizing what it means to be alive! The intent of salvation and service has never been to "block" emotion or to create a culture that is robotic, legalistic… unfeeling and cold. In fact, I believe the exact opposite is true. God wants us to feel and to LIVE (3 John 1:2)! But what he does not want is a people who are "ruled by" or who "live by" those feelings. He has not called us into *emotionalism*. Emotionalism in the life of a believer is indeed sinful. This is where danger lies. **We must remember this truth:** In the life of a believer, Christ must become Lord over our emotions as we are led by the Spirit. In addition, our emotions are supposed to flow from a *pure heart* under the subjection of "the mind of Christ." This is the healthy place, the God place in which we can meet emotion in our dreams.

Ezekiel 36:24-28 NIV says, *"For I will take you <u>out</u> of the nations; I will gather you from all the countries and bring you back into your own land. I <u>will sprinkle clean water on you, and you will be clean;</u> I will cleanse you from all your impurities and from all your idols. <u>I will give you a new heart and put a new spirit in you; I will remove from you your heart of stone and give you a heart of flesh. And I will put my Spirit in you and move you to follow my decrees and be careful to keep my laws</u>. Then you will live in the land I gave your ancestors; you will be my people, and I will be your God."*

Emotions in dreams released by God will generally assist the dreamer with unveiling: (1) the weight or heaviness of the Word; (2) the depth of Christ's compassion; (3) the need for brokenness, humility and submission to Christ; (4) the cry for reconciliation of all kinds; (5) the sovereignty of God; (6) the cry for compassion, intercession and prayer; and/or (7) the fear of the Lord. To verify this, go back through the dreams and visions revealed in scripture… and consider them with new eyes. **These truths eliminate the perverseness of erotic dreams or fantasy, dreams that release terror in the style of nightmares, or other signs of impurity.** Dreams released by God follow his patterns, his ways and his heart for reconciliation. As with all things, dreams should be weighed prophetically to be SURE that they are of God. Even in the midst of understanding emotion in dreams, the "sons of God" must refer back to scripture and solid scriptural examples and patterns for understanding.

From the perspective of wisdom in this area, I must say that most emotionally-laden, intense dreams may not God-centered. Rather, they are fueled by the soul. So be very careful with what is shared here. In no way do we need babes or prophetic people who are still in their maturation process misunderstanding what is shared here. As a result, I strongly recommend dreamers who experience "emotionally rich" dreams to walk through them with SEASONED believers who understand dream interpretation, and the things of the Spirit.

I would be cautious of constant dream encounters *saturated* in emotion. For those who do move in purity in this area, the emotional aspect can be instrumental in your life. For a prophetic scribe who is an actor, for example, they may develop a vision and heart for their character through encounters in the realm of dreams. As authors and writers, it is not unusual to develop a perspective on characters in ones plays, books, movie scripts, etc. through dream realm encounters. For some scribes, the emotion observed or experienced is as critical as the images and/or words themselves.

Don't forget that God also deals with us personally in our dreams. We talked about this earlier. Those encounters can be overwhelmingly filled with emotion and waves of healing. I was driven to write many poems, plays and songs from those personal encounters. During this season of my life, I also walked in intense accountability in this area. Again, this is the one area where we must exude an extreme amount of caution in "Holy Spirit." However, to ignore this area – and not mention it at all – would not be fair to those scribes who have sought God concerning what is going on in them; but have been too afraid or ashamed to discuss it openly. I pray that you realize that you are not alone… and that God can and does speak SCRIBALLY through your emotions in dreams.

TRUST WHERE HE LEADS

Make me know your ways, Adonai, teach me your paths.
Guide me in your truth, and teach me;
for you are the God who saves me.
~ Psalm 5:4-5

TRUSTING THE DREAM REALM

Noone of our experiences supersede the written word of God. While we have indeed journeyed into the supernatural realm of dreams and visions in this book, God's word always remains supreme. I strongly believe that the best way to judge the validity of a dream or a vision is by ensuring that it lines up with the *heart and mind of God* as it is revealed in the scriptures from a good, solid Bible. Hear me when I say this: There can be no exception to this rule. If what is revealed through the dream encounter does not reflect the very person of God... Christ, it is likely you have crossed into or are crossing into dangerous territory. Prophetic people grow to understand this fully. Dreams, just like prophecy, must bear witness to what God has already spoken and revealed. Revelation EXPANDS... and brings clarity to the Word of God. **The dream realm cannot create a new doctrine, a new Gospel.** The types of dreams represented in the Bible are wide and broad. They move from simple and extreme to downright weird! Yet, their interpretations, those interpreted for us in scripture, clearly represent God's ancient and presently relevant ideology. It becomes clear that the realm of visions and dreams are not only released by God, but subject to His pattern for revealing truth that relies on what has *already* been spoken. Christ made this clear in his declarations that absolutely everything He said or did mirrored the mind of God.

Every son has the responsibility of representing the Father well. In the same way, every son understands that trusting the dream realm begins with fully trusting God, the ONLY dream giver. It is when we forget this foundation that we cross into the unknown, the stuff of "self" and even into the darkness that reveals the doctrine of demons. The litmus test of all things supernatural is God's Word. We must be *diligent* dividers of truth.

2 Timothy 3:16-17 AMP says, *"All Scripture is God-breathed [given by divine inspiration] and is profitable for instruction, for conviction [of sin], for correction [of error and restoration to obedience], **for training in righteousness [learning to live in conformity to God's will, both publicly and privately—behaving honorably with personal integrity and moral courage];** so that the man of God may be complete and proficient, outfitted and thoroughly equipped for every good work."*

Finally, having a word or insight that "bears witness" with one's spirit, does not always mean that it bears witness with God's Word. You see, if your own soul is troubled, questioning, messed up, mixed up or unaccountable; then that can filter into the interpretation of spiritual things. I strongly suggest that the SAME pattern used to judge prophecy be applied to the final interpretation of dreams – even those that we receive concerning ourselves whenever possible **(1 Corinthians 14:29)**. Again, this is my suggestion. If I fail to share this with you, then I am not fulfilling my role in your life at this moment as an instructor. While there are many God-centered forums, books and teachings to assist with understanding dreams, visions and dream interpretation, I have yet to identify any that focus on "scribal dream mastery" for those who are "called or commanded" to write and record out of the dream realm. In addition, nearly every dream course I have encountered encourage writing down the dream but the information is very basic. Those resources do not tap into the *office* of the scribe. I believe this book has changed that for us.

WHY TRUST THE DREAM REALM?

Not all scribes will be scribes who dream. Failing to acknowledge that this is a vital way that God chooses to speak to me, would grossly hinder my purposes as a scribe. If you have been in denial, I do hope you have come to a point of awakening. Failing to recognize the value of the scribal realm could result in shutting down or closing off a critical aspect of your spiritual growth and maturity. You would be denying a significant aspect of your identity in Christ.

It was NECESSARY that I learn to trust the dream realm. This very book would not be here... in this moment... without my personal realm of dreams. Earlier, I shared a picture with you concerning my trip to the Library of Heaven. Guess what? That image is one of many that I have captured from supernatural dream journeys. They are also a part of some phenomenal revelation God has given me for another book. In addition, I cannot forget that as a result of my obedience many scribes who connect with this message will be unlocked, released and set free. So if someone asked me this question: "Why trust the dream realm?" I would answer, "I trust the dream realm because it is God's preferred vehicle for speaking to me concerning my purpose and destiny in Him." It's that simple.

Like Habakkuk, I have learned to LOOK TO SEE what GOD WILL SAY TO ME... and WHAT ANSWER I AM TO GIVE. **The dream realm has ANSWERS directly from God and the hosts of heaven!**

We should trust the dream realm:

- Because it is a place where God deeply imparts His Word into His sons. **(The Book of Ezekiel, Ezekiel 3:1)**

- Because it is one of God's chosen places for meeting with us for the purpose of impartation and blessing. **(Genesis 46:2; Genesis 28:10-17; 1 Kings 3:5-15; 2 Corinthians 12:2)**

- Because God uses it to release detailed instructions, understanding, vision and insight concerning his will and his plans. **(Judges 7:12-15; Ezekiel 37; Genesis 31:10-11; Matthew 1:18-24; Habakkuk 1:1, 2:2-3)**

- Because it can be the VERY CENTER of prayer and intercession in your life. I think this might be another book! **(Psalm 42:8; Col. 4:12)**

- Because God uses it to bring strong correction, direction, clarity, and even to instill the fear of the Lord in His sons and those who do not know Him. **(Acts 7:30-32; Job 33:14-18; Matthew 27:19; Judges 7:12-15; Genesis 40; Genesis 41)**

- Because future events are revealed by God that will assist in our preparation for whatever is to come. **(Ezekiel 12:27; Daniel 8l Amos 1; Isaiah 21:2; Judges 7:13-15; Revelation; Genesis 41:1-7; Genesis 37:9; Luke 1:5-23; Genesis 15:1, Matthew 1:20; Matthew 2:13)**

- Because it reveals the activities of heaven and its impact in the earth, and in the lives of God's people. **(Zechariah 6:1-8; Isaiah 6:1-8; Acts 2:1-4; Exodus 24:9-10; Exodus 33:23; 2 Chronicles 18:18; Ezekiel 1:26; Revelation 4:2)**

- Because it is a key method in which God warns and protects His people, relay His will or pronounce His judgments. **(Matthew 27:19; Matthew 2:12; Zechariah 5:2-4; Amos 9:1; Amos 8:1-6; Daniel 4:5; Ezekiel 8:2-4; Genesis 20:1-7; Genesis 40)**

- Because God uses it to bring forth healing, deliverance, freedom and to give life to his people. **(Acts 9:3; Ezekiel 37:1-10; Acts 2:4)**

- Help other people, nations or obtain the help you need. **(Acts 9:10-11; Acts16:9; Acts 10:1-7)**

- Reveal the counsel of God, bring correction, and to protect His people. **(Acts 22:18; Judges 7:13-15; Matthew 2:12; Matthew 2:13; Genesis 15:1; Job 33:11-17)**

- Reveal the secrets and mysteries of the Kingdom. **(Daniel 2:28; Daniels 2:19)**

- Reveal our assignments, callings, destiny and purpose. **(Numbers 12:6; Matthew 2:13; Acts 16:9; 2 Corinthians 12:1-6; Acts 18:9; 1 Samuel 3:2-15; Genesis 46:2; Genesis 37:5, 9; 1 Samuel 1:3; Ezekiel 3)**

Scribes, I want to courage you to go through the scriptures listed above. Pay attention to not only the specific verse highlighted, but also the context in which the vision or the dream was given. Observe the posture of the dreamer and their interactions in their specific dream realm. By doing so, you will gain valuable insight into your own dream life. This process will be instrumental in assisting you with discerning what is of God and what is not in the days and weeks to come. This exercise is profitable whether you are new to your scribal realm or seasoned. Father said this to me plainly: "No son is exempt from deception in the times in which we live. We must remain vigilant in our pursuit to embrace God's Word and ways. The best way to maintain that vigilance is by knowing His Word."

A PLACE OF PRAYER & TRUST

I would like to argue that the question Habakkuk presented to God was a type of prayer. It was a pondering in His heart that needed a response. Habakkuk's intercession was along the lines of a lament, similar to Jeremiah's pleas in Lamentations that were drenched in passion, sorrow and deep emotion. Whether knowingly or unknowingly, we incubate those types of prayers in our hearts constantly – whether they are vocalized, kept silently or linger in our subconscious.

Walking out this process called life can be beautiful. Like me, I know you can recall times in which you felt alive and enjoyed every opportunity given to you to breathe deeply. And more than likely, you also know what it is like to endure sorrow so great that even expressing the heaviness and struggle seems unbearable. Without out a doubt, the ability to move through the good and bad days as a believer has been rooted in my relationship with Christ and developing a reliance on the gift of comfort that comes from Holy Spirit.

Habakkuk's heart was full of questions in the midst of great anguish. His response: He stood before God presenting his question from His heart. **There is absolutely no indication – at least in the story of Habakkuk – that HE SPOKE His question.** Pause here for a moment. This is what I want you to draw from these truths at this point: **God _heard_ the cry of Habakkuk's spirit and the anguish of his soul.** Remember, the Lord says He **HEARS AND SEES** the meditation of our heart in the Psalms. That also means he responds. There is no way we, as sons, could ask for bread and then receive stones from Him.

Whether we realize it or not, we are ALWAYS questioning God. Our spirit and our soul are filled with the ponderings we carry concerning God, the condition of this world and even the things we carry in our own soul! It is in this DIMENSION that many answers to prayer are given and calls to intercession are opened up to us by way of dreams and visions. Our spirit man retains so much more information than we realize… or could ever imagine.

I cannot begin to tell you how tormented I was when I entered the Kingdom. I grew up in a very volatile environment – void of the nurture and care of both mother and father. The things I endured in my life were so severe that they left me bitter, angry, full of rage… and dis-fragmented. Yet, when I entered the Kingdom…. I was plunged into such a deep and vivid dream realm. As I shared before, I would wake up from those dreams writing and crying like a person who had lost their mind. What I didn't share was that some of those dreams were EXTREMELY healing. Like many of you who may be reading this book, I saw those dream encounters back them from the perspective of a movie… not a place of real healing and deliverance. I know now that those healing encounters were just as much a reality as the pages in this book.

Today, I can tell you that GOD WAS LISTENING TO MY SPIRIT and the CRY OF MY SOUL. He was meeting me in my dream realm to "pray over me." Holy Spirit was assisting me IN MY DREAM REALM with approaching the throne room of God in boldness… in truth.

People of God, I didn't know how to pray for myself. I was a brand new believer who was in pain ALL THE TIME. I could feel the presence of God but I could also feel death all around me as I fought suicide, depression and had reached a point in my life in which I had to face my "demons" so to speak if I was every going to move forward. I was so ashamed of my past and all the secrets that I carried that I could not verbally articulate all the trauma in my heart. Nor did I want to do that or had the strength to do it. My trust issues were so severe it would be another four years before I shared the most traumatizing aspects of my journey with anyone. I am not telling you this for myself, but to help you understand one of the most BEAUTIFUL aspects of the scribal realm of dreams and visions. Because I recorded so many of these experiences, I can look back now… and rightly interpret God's work in my heart, my soul.

In this one dream, I was running barefoot along a paved road on a pitch black night. I was completely alone and afraid. There were buildings burning an exploding on my left side and I was trying desperately to get away from them. At the same time, there were these deep holes in the shape of graves chiseled into the asphalt. As I ran, I had to jump over each one them… or else I would fall in. As the buildings burned, they would break up and fall in my direction – one after the other. I had no time to pause, to look back or to do anything other than run. When I awoke, I had this overwhelming feeling that my life was at stake… and that I was in danger of dying. The fear was so strong I could barely suppress the shaking and the tears when I woke up with this urgent command to record it.

With the help of a prophet, I was able to get this interpretation: "Beloved, keep running even in the midst of the darkness. I am with you and you are chasing me. The buildings represent your past and the consuming fire is my spirit as I burn down everything that will dare remind you of your past. Your bare feet touching the ground indicates that this journey will not be easy. There will be bruising and pain, but I have called you to stay the course, to run the race well. The coffin sized holes in the ground represent the traps in your mind that can easily pull you back into the darkness, burying you in the very grave that I have delivered you from. Beloved, you much jump over the graves even as the buildings fall. You cannot give up, because I am your prize and you will overcome. As long as you choose me, I will cover you." This prophetic interpretation was preceded by this passage of scripture, **Rev. 12:11**.

From this perspective, you can actually see that this "dark dream" was actually a visual, prophetic prayer released to me in the scribal realm of dreams and visions. God HEARD ME… even though I did not speak it out. He RESPONSED to me… even though I never directly asked the question. Even if I did not "knowingly approach the throne boldly," my spirit was open and understood how to respond with Holy Spirit leading.

Hebrews 4:16 NIV says, *"For we do not have a high priest who is unable to sympathize with our weaknesses, but we have one who was tempted in every way that we are, yet was without sin. Let us then approach the throne of grace with confidence, so that we may receive mercy and find grace to help us in our time of need."*

We can have demands in the Spirit that we are unaware of that God will answer in our dreams. Among the most significant of these demands is answered prayers and healing encounters specifically geared toward working out our soul's salvation with fear and trembling. The manifestation of prayer in dreams takes on many, many forms. I earnestly believe that no one person has the full revelation of what this looks like. Why? Because God meets each one of us in our place of need and equipping. The potential of the scribal realm of dreams and visions with God is endless.

I specifically wanted to talk about those inward prayers or petitions that reside in our spirit as part of this section of the book. But as we have learned from Habakkuk, we can also formulate questions in our heart and carry them with us in our dreams. In addition, our dream experiences can include:

- Engaging in prayer in our dreams for ourselves, individuals, nations, etc.;

- Praying for or over specific people in our dreams, including administering healing and deliverance;

- Seeing our prayers answered in dreams, and awaking with revelation, knowledge and understanding concerning specific prayer requests;

- Seeing ourselves laying prostrate or in varying prayer, praise or worship postures in very specific environments;

- Waking up directly out of the sleep state praying in one's heavenly language or with a known language; or

- Waking up with burdens and oracles to pray for specific nations, people, places or situations.

This isn't intended to be a complete list. It is my hope, however, that you will find yourself open to how God will use you with all kinds of prayers and petitions! There is absolutely no way the Lord would open us this realm so profoundly and not use it to fulfill every single aspect of Isaiah 61 in your life or in the lives of others. We must also remember that when we PRAY… there is an expectation of clarity and understanding. Armed with what we have discussed here scribes of the King, you can also purpose yourself to be in a prayerful place at all times so that when you enter the scribal realm of dreams and visions… you are completely ready to receive what God has in store for you. You can trust the "prayer place" in the scribal realm of dreams and visions.

DREAM SAFEGUARDS

Ecclesiastes 5:3 NIV says, *"A dream comes when there are many cares, and many words mark the speech of a fool."*

Trusting the dream realm isn't easy, especially since our dreams can come from our soul, especially when we are under a great deal of stress and pressure. Trust me, I know this well. These kinds of dreams are fueled by the cares of life. As we have previously discussed, some dreams can come from a mixture of others influences as well – especially among prophetic people – and drip with great confusion. I can't say this enough: "We must be cautious in this area, careful not to exhort the dream realm or the dreams over God's Word **(2 Timothy 3:16-17)**."

Rather, we MUST weigh our dreams by the Word of God as we would with any prophetic declaration. The prophetic exercise we walked through earlier is an excellent tool to help those firmly rooted in the Lord filter their dreams. There are no guarantees or promises that come with that exercise per se, but I do know it may help establish our dream pattern. With anything in the prophetic, we must come to a place of stability, maturity and clarity within our own process.

This is, perhaps, why I am so concerned with our continued supernatural development. The 21st Century ushered in a fresh, revitalizing dynamic that is building upon the good of the previous moves of God exponentially – especially as it relates to apostolic and prophetic ministry. It is pressing the Body from a place of generalities into extreme areas of mastery – especially as it relates to secrets and mysteries surrounding the prophetic scribe. What makes this dispensation different, however, is that it is becoming increasingly difficult to resurrect old patterns and apply them to present day.

As a result, it is critical that we tap into every significant resource God has opened up to us to explore our unique identities. It's been over 10 years since the Lord released a word to me that there was a *scribal anointing* upon the land. But as I look around today, I see the manifestation of that Word absolutely everywhere. We went from dry bones to a scribal revolution in a 10-year span – especially in the areas surrounding creative scribal ministry. As our Father continues to unfold that prophecy from 2005, we must TRUST every prophetic tool at our disposal to develop our calling. Why? Because we are still in the midst of a newly chartered, yet to be fully explored territory surrounding scribal ministry in the realm of the Spirit. And we, scribes of the King, have been in the trenches building since God opened it up. This School of the Scribe is pioneering.

The key to moving forward remains in pursuing pure ministry – ministry without any motive other than pleasing God. Otherwise, the revelation shared here can become convoluted and twisted. " Let us not be found in this place.

Prophetic Scribes, I believe that there are different "realms in the area of dreams and visions" for every believer. I believe there are realms specific to every type of ministry found or revealed in scripture – whether it is the ministry of helps, ministry in the visual arts, ministry to the abandoned and abused; or to musicians, psalmists and dancers. If God can count every hair on our head, capture our tears, sorrows in a bottle, hear and see every meditation and thought then surely he can STILL speak to us through a dream or a vision.

As growth continues, I believe prophetic scribes will begin to see the dream realm as:

- A place of apostolic and prophetic incubation.

- An intercessory chamber or board room.

- A war room designed to unveil uncommon strategy.

- A portal to ascend and descend into high places.

- The convening of a heavenly courtroom.

- A place of meeting, interaction and exchange between angels and men.

- A place of divine intervention between God and man.

- A portal for transitioning from natural death into eternal life like Stephen.

- A heavenly view into what is and what is to come.

- A place of spiritual training and growth in life and the prophetic.

- A place of peace and comfort.

- A place of healing, deliverance and breakthrough.

- A place of increasing belief, trust and love.

- A place of natural and spiritual preparation or preparedness.

To fully tap into what God has for us here we must learn to effectively and efficiently steward the scribal realm of dreams and visions to avoid walking into dangerous territory. Certain safeguards MUST be put in place and are non-negotiable.

A safeguard is a *security* measure or precaution that protects or defends something we deem to be essential and precious. WITHOUT these safeguards, it is truly UNWISE to place one's trust in the realm of visions and dreams.

Here are four essential safeguards that must be in the life of a prophetic scribe who lives in the scribal realm of dreams and visions. We have talked about some of them, but now it is time to hammer them into our hearing. **They are simple, practical and again NON-NEGOTIABLE... regardless of how much you know, how long you have been saved or where you perceive yourself to be in ministry or in life.** Remember, **Matthew 13:52** reminds the scribe that he or she must be *"masters of the house."* In other words, we must steward what is received into our hearts and what we perceive concerning our giftings, callings and purpose in the Kingdom.

These safeguards area as follows:

1. **Read and study God's word regularly using a solid Bible.** This is the first level of stewardship. Your reading and study, however,

should be focused on knowing God... not just preparing for a sermon or seeking out revelation. Consider using a Bible reading plan for this initiative and setting up a reading time every single day to feed your soul and spirit – whether it is 10 minutes or an hour. For study, I would suggest a King James Bible Version and a Strong's Concordance along with another Bible of your choice. That way, you can do basic research that will assist in getting to the original meaning of the text. Finally, remember that if the Word is not being poured into you, it will not flow out of you. We must posture our study surrounding Christ's declaration: *I only do what I see the Father do, and only speak what I hear the Father speak.* God's word cleanses the soul, strengthens us in understanding who He is and what He desires. It is essential to helping us distinguish between God's voice, our voice, the voice of a stranger and the voice of the adversary. Without this essential component, it is impossible to TRUST the authenticity of the dream realm.

2. **You must pursue a prayerful life.** It is critical that you spend time in personal prayer—just you and the Father. This is our primary means of intimately communicating with God and receiving from Him. This part of your life does not have to be overly dramatic or religious, but it does need to be consistent, stable, earnest and sincere. If you struggle in this area, simply ask Holy Spirit to guide you. Pray the Lord's Prayer, pray scriptures that address areas of growth in your life, the psalms or other passages. Exercise your heavenly language if you have it. In fact, begin by asking the Lord give you wisdom and understanding in the scriptures. Without a solid prayer life in addition to Word intake, it is impossible to TRUST the authenticity of one's dream realm.

3. **Be accountable in the Word and in your prayer life through intimate fellowship with other believers.** Deep confusion exists in isolation and same-level fellowship (hanging out with people just like you and who do not challenge you in the Word apostolically). Consistent fellowship is critical among the people of God. We need to be accountable for our how we live, able to ask questions about the Word of God and His ways in student-teacher relationships, not just peer-to-peer. I firmly believe that God has a safe place for EVERY believer to grow and gain insight in simplicity and truth. In this, I am speaking of stable relationship… not hopping from person to person, group to group or congregation to congregation. Find some consistency in who you receive from.

4. **Record every single dream and vision God commands.** Obedience in the scribal realm of dreams and visions is extremely important. Every act of obedience reveals a deeper level of trust and unlocks greater revelation and understanding. Being attentive to the urgent call or request is at the center of the prophetic scribe's ministry. Remain obedient.

There are clearly more areas that can be posted here; however, I firmly believe that these are the most critical safeguards. Scribes, let's face it. If you lack the first two points, you run this risk of having an unstable, unreliable… soul-directed dream life.

YOUR DREAM TRACK RECORD

I have mentored many scribes and prophetic people – many of whom range from occasional to prolific dreamers. Among the things I longed to drill into them was the value of **"being obedient and consistent"** concerning the scribal instructions given specific to them. Without BOTH it is impossible to develop any type of mastery in the scribal realm of dream of visions beyond common, expected experiences. Every act of obedience in the midst of consistency pushes us into deeper realms of comprehension, and ultimately results in extremely mature revelation that is supported by biblically sound wisdom. Just because a pattern works with one specific dreamer does not mean that pattern will work with you. Trust me, I know this from experience. Sometimes, you have to work out your "own" unique process even in the midst of tools that are provided.

While it is not said word for word in the scriptures, it is clear that Habakkuk was a *disciplined* and *trained* seer. He did not simply show up on the seen with those mature skills and techniques that we observe. He knew and was experienced in how to posture himself to enter the scribal realm of dreams and visions; and how to interact with God in that sphere. Prophetic scribes, Habakkuk presents us with a view of what obedience and consistency might look like… and the kind of mysteries that unfold when we mature in our calling. Every prophetic scribes owes it to themselves to dig out every treasure hidden in the midst of their calling.

If I had not been diligent in my dream recording process, I would NEVER be able to share this revelation with you today. This insight is a direct result of building a "dream realm track record with God." I realize now more than ever that my dream encounters were not simply about "getting an interpretation" of a dream or a vision – although that is critically important. It was about learning to hear God beyond what was normal to me… through the understanding of my **personal** dream process. It was also about TRUSTING my personal dream realm, and navigating key aspects of my life based on what I learned. LISTEN, THE PROCESS – **YOUR UNIQUE PROCESS** - IS SO IMPORTANT! As dreamers, we must begin to shift our thinking in this direction. It was about another level of walking in the Spirit with the Father and developing a "different kind" of track record with Him.

Personally, I can go on-and-on with these personal truths. I reached a point in my walk in which God knew that He could TRUST ME with what I was given. He knew that my "track record" was authentic. Merriam-Webster defines "track record" as a combination of "things that someone or something has done or achieved in the past regarded especially as a way to judge what that person or thing is likely to do in the future."[30]

In other words, your consistency and obedience to a thing – better known as faithfulness – is an indicator of your future actions. So, if you have a proven track record of completing or following through with what is before you then, more than likely, you can be trusted with more or greater. However, if you are found to be unfaithful in that thing... you develop a poor track record and run the risk of being trusted with little. Remember the parable of the talent in **Matthew 25**? It is about faithfulness, stewardship and building a reliable track record.

I had to live this process long before I could put together the numerous notes from my dream encounters into book format. For years, I only saw the dream realm as a place to receive and get interpretations that would direct my life or help direct the body in a prophetic capacity. Oh how limited that type of thinking was! Believe it or not, I didn't start out obedient. I was a horrible steward with a horrible track record in the beginning of my journey. One day, I decided to steward my dream realm for 40 solid days without interruption. Let me tell you, I moved into a different place spiritually... one in which I could see and experience the benefits of being consistent.

My scribal journey proved that small instructions are indeed "bricks" being carefully, supernaturally placed along the walls of our foundation with God. Without each brick and the mortar that fills in the gaps, we end up with houses full of holes... space for vermin to enter and wreak havoc.

---

[30] Merriam-Webster Online, *Track Record*, http://www.merriam-webster.com/dictionary/track%20record

Scribes of the King, there's something to be said about obeying God in everything. I am not telling you to be perfect! Lord knows we are daily being perfected. I am saying give God your best and watch destiny and purpose unfold.

REVELATION RUNNERS

"...so that a herald may run with it."
~ Habakkuk 2:2b

GOD'S HERALDS

Habakkuk 2:2 NIV reads, *"Write down the revelation and make it plain on tablets **so that a herald may run with it.**"*

In Scripture both angels and humans are employed as heralds, "and on occasions even specific events may herald future happenings."[31] In this context, the term herald is represented as a noun and a verb. So as we discuss its scriptural meaning, we must see the term from both perspectives.

As a noun, a herald is best defined as a person officially employed to deliver a message, like a mailman or courier - one who proclaims a message or paves the way for a promised event. Another term closely associated with a herald from this viewpoint is a crier or a "town crier," an official who makes announcements before a court of justice. In our English dictionaries, a herald is described as "a royal or official messenger, especially one representing a monarch in an ambassadorial capacity during wartime; and a person or thing that precedes or comes before as in a forerunner or harbinger."[32] In this sense, many of us – simply as sons of God - can claim the role of herald. As a verb, herald is the act of announcing with the intent of reaching as many people with a specific message as possible. The actual role of an announcer would fit the bill here. Then, there is the perspective of the message itself operating *as a herald*. For example, key prophesies in the Old Covenant heralded (foreshadowed or foretold) the coming of Christ. When we look at Habakkuk's oracle or burden, it heralded God's intent toward the people of Judah. In other words, the message that is released also announces or proclaims itself.

---

[31] Martin H. Manser, Dictionary of Bible Themes, *Herald*,
https://www.biblegateway.com/resources/dictionary-of-bible-themes/5335-herald
[32] Dictionary.com, *Herald*, http://www.dictionary.com/browse/herald

The Holman Bible Dictionary uses the following examples to convey these meanings: "The herald of **Daniel 3:4** was responsible for publicizing the king's law and the penalty of disobedience. Noah is described as a herald of righteousness **(2 Peter 2:5)**, that is, one who announced God's requirements. Paul was appointed as a herald or preacher of the gospel. **1 Timothy 2:5-7** outlines Paul's message as the uniqueness of God, Christ's unique role as mediator between God and humanity, and Christ's death as ransom. **2 Timothy 1:9-11** outlines Paul's gospel as the good news that God has given grace by sending Christ who abolished death and brought life."[33]

In Habakkuk, I believe the understanding of herald as a noun and as a verb apply in our discussion in both a natural and spiritual sense. The passage describes heralds as believers who are so impacted and stirred by the *weight and urgency* of the message the prophet released that they are *compelled* by Holy Spirit to announce or proclaim that message to as many people as possible AND to cause that message to be demonstrative in the midst of their own lives. It also infers that there are those who will grasp "certain" pronouncements and literally live them out. Those who hear will believe what God has said and act accordingly.

The story of the woman at the well provides another strong example of a herald in **John 4:1-29**. If you are not familiar with this account, please review these passages. Then, meditate on **verses 28-29** which read: *"Then the woman left her water jar, **and went into the city and began telling the people,** Come, see a man who told me all the things that I have done! Can this be the Christ (the Messiah, the Anointed)?"*

Why is this significant? Because it reveals that God already has a predetermined audience for the messages He releases into the earth – whether written, recorded or demonstrated. It proves that we do not have

---

[33] Holman Bible Dictionary Online, *Herald*, Broadman & Holman: 1991, http://www.studylight.org/dictionaries/hbd/view.cgi?number=T2723

control over "who gets" the scribe's message or who "runs" with it. It reminds us that how one person publishes their scribal project might not be the way you are called to publish yours – and that is absolutely okay. It is critical that every single "prophetic scribe" follows the exact details God gives them. What works for one person is not necessarily the prescription for another.

Remember, Habakkuk's oracles were never delivered to any *specific* person or audience directly; he never spoke the oracles out loud to anyone; and while he was commanded to write them, he was not responsible for their direct distribution. Instead, the distribution was set by God himself and was dependent upon "heralds" either obtaining and delivering copies of what he wrote or simply carrying the accuracy of the oracle to others by word-of-mouth.

I keep mentioning this over and over because it is so strategically prophetic! For present day scribes, this is an amazing observation. It literally confirms that every scribe must seek to find His or her own instructions – whether it relates to a written prophecy, poem, novel, devotion, comic book, greeting card or book of instruction. If you are a scribe, and your scribal project only "seems to reach" a limited audience – do not get discouraged! There might be one person amid that limited group who needs that message or who will spread that message to others.

The most critical message here is this: "If our Father in Heaven has indeed placed His message in your hand, then rest assured that IT WILL REACH EVERY SINGLE SOUL THAT IS ASSIGNED TO IT at the appointed time – as long as you are obedient and steadfast in fulfilling the directives given to you!"

Success in the system of this world is always based on "what is visible" and "financially measurable." This is not the truth in God's economy. Look at us right now! Habakkuk had absolutely no way of knowing that what He wrote would be used as extensively as it is today in our journey to know Christ. He didn't know that one day the Apostle Paul would obtain a greater revelation from His message on faith. He didn't know that we would be learning about scribal ministry from His example! Whatever perceptions we may or may not have about publishing are CRUSHED under the reality of this truth: God is the only one who directs the prophetic scribe. Our scribal process is supernatural. This is a difficult concept to grasp for most prophetic scribes, especially when success as a writer, playwright, administrator, orator, etc. is important to the person. Sometimes, this might not be God's direction and then, sometimes it is. If the Lord desires a certain message to reach the masses and ignite the nations through a mainstream initiative, He will surely lead his scribes in that direction; or at the appointed time He will cause that completed work to be made known. If the Lord has preserved a message for a remnant, He will also provide instructions for distributing that message to that specific population of people. No direction or directive is greater than the other when it is directed by the Lord! Scribes of the King, I pray that this is made known in your heart. The lesson is that we follow our specific course.

One of the greatest lies ever told is that WE must make it happen. God's truth declares that HE will make it happen as we follow His every lead.

THE APPOINTED TIME

Habakkuk 2:3 AMP says, *"For the revelation awaits **an appointed** time; it speaks of the end and will not prove false. Though it linger, wait for it; it will certainly come and will not delay."*

I was called into the office of an apostle back in 2008. I was not walking in it, but God's apostolic grace was upon me… in plain sight. I did not desire it, but other apostles and leaders simply began addressing me as such – against my will really. Quite honestly, it made me extremely uncomfortable. In this particular year, I was… perhaps, at the peak of one of the most spiritually devastating trials I had ever faced in my spiritual life. My faith in the local church was wavering; and I was developing this deep intolerance for religion or should I say church as usual. I didn't know from one day to the next who was for me or against me – even in my home church and in my own home. Some of the closest relationships that I had were disintegrating right before my eyes; and the ministry I had committed my life too was being undermined by people whom I admired and trusted most. I was fighting for my life, naturally and spiritually. The level of misunderstandings and betrayal were monumental. For a long time, I thought I had a target on my back that read: "Here I am! Do your worst!" Then, there was a final blow… that was so devastating it took me years of healing to rise above it.

Other trials have come, but without a doubt – none have compared to that season in my life. It was in this dark time that I heard Father say to me: *"Endure. My glory will shine through all that you have overcome and everything that I have promised you will indeed come to pass."* In that moment, I knew there was an **appointed time for me**. After all, I was still standing. The only thing I knew to do with certainty was pursue His presence and glean joy from every moment that presented itself. It would be 2010 before I finally obtained a major breakthrough through a healing encounter in Kansas City, Missouri, and began moving past that ordeal and trusting God in people again. Truly, that was an appointed time. God sent a team of pastors to undergird my journey. In that same year, the Lord connected with my first apostle in this new season of my life… who helped me transition in to the apostolic in 2011. It was as if I had spiritually advanced three decades in the span of just three years.

It was then that I began having more of these vibrant, life-giving, restorative dream encounters with angels holding scrolls and swords. My dream pattern began changing. They began showing up in nearly every dream – wielding military attire and swords! I have shared one of those images on the next page.

Luke 22:43-44 NIV, *"An angel from heaven appeared to him and strengthened him. And being in anguish, he prayed more earnestly…"*

Yes, I know angels do not really look like that drawing by biblical descriptions, but in my personal scribal realm of dreams and visions, this is how they present themselves. Aspects of my interpretation of their presence indicated:

- They were prepared for battle.

- These angels were there to strengthen me.

- The scrolls in their hands were like swords and shields.

- They were guarding "me."

- They were guarding the revelation in the scrolls.

- The three scrolls were specifically for me.

- The scrolls were critical to my identity and purpose;

- They were delivering the scrolls.

- There were the keepers of the scrolls.

- The scrolls were unsealed.

- Confirmation that God was indeed leading and directing me.

- Confirmation that God was protecting and covering me.

I experienced dream encounters like this for months! And each time, I'd awaken with a little more strength to continue this journey and tons of poetry and spoken word surrounding injustice and the Kingdom! My dream realm – in this season - became a lifeline for me when it seemed outwardly that there was nothing else to really build me in faith and belief. Shortly after these particular types of dreams ended, I wrote another instrumental book for prophetic scribes and worshippers.

Yes, I know this might seem like a rabbit trail in the midst of this book, but I want you to grasp that "your appointed time" is tied to your ability to **overcome and endure** while remaining in obedience – even when you feel as if there is nothing else in you to give. If I had a dollar for every moment I thought this "scribal" ministry thing was a waste of time... I'd be a millionaire today! Seriously. I had to learn SEE for myself that this was God even amid the people who told me it emphatically, "You are on the wrong course. This is not real ministry." **My dream life TOLD A DIFFERENT STORY! My dream life opened doors to appointed times and were revealing APPOINTED TIMES to come!** My visions DEMANDED to be written. I could not afford to faint... even though I didn't understand God's plan or appointed time.

Habakkuk did not faint. He did the only thing that he knew to do: Stand on his rampart. Then, look to see what God would say to him and what answer he would give. We have no idea HOW MANY TIMES IN HIS LIFE HE HAD TO WALK THIS WAY! What we do know, however, is that He did complete the journey, releasing the oracle that he struggled so hard to see.

Let's transition.

The biblical understanding of appointed times is primarily associated with feast days – times set aside on the Hebraic calendar for certain feasts and festivals. From this perspective, these appointed times were immovable and set to achieve some very specific purpose as established by God. From a broader viewpoint, an appointed time is a time *known only by God* concerning when something will take place, be fulfilled or sealed that He alone has preordained. Another excellent example of this can be seen in the passage below:

Matthew 24:35-36 AMP says: *"Heaven and earth [as now known] will pass away, but My words will not pass away. **But of that [exact] day and hour no one knows,** not even the angels of heaven, nor the Son [in His humanity], **but the Father alone.**"*

As prophetic scribes, we must realize that while God uses us to release His will in the earth, He is not obligated to give us every detail concerning his plans. Based on scripture, He enjoys unfolding things before us. Personally, I really believe God enjoys watching our amazement and seeing us rise in triumph and joy at the fulfillment of His Word, promises. **Deuteronomy 29:29** tells us plainly that God *owns* all **secrets, mysteries**; and that what He gives to us **is ours and for our generations forever.** Clearly, what God shares with us is on a need to know basis and is released at times that He alone sets. Our duty as scribes will always encompass some or all areas of recording, writing, releasing, publishing, distributing or teaching.

When we think about it, waiting for the fulfillment of an oracle, a promise or a prophetic word is *expected* in our faith journey just as it was in the faith journey of the biblical patriarchs and matriarchs across the Old and New Covenants. One of the most profound examples of this can be found in **Isaiah 7:14** where the virgin birth of Christ is prophesied. This prophecy was not fulfilled in Isaiah's lifetime. Does this mean that the prophecy was false? Absolutely not! It simply meant that the time of its fulfillment was not yet at hand. This presents a plethora of questions that the prophetic scribe may want to ask. For example, what if one of the prophecies you receive from the dream realm is set to come to pass in another generation? Listen, there are believers throughout history who were looked upon as insignificant... and centuries later their impact is continuing to be felt. During their lifetime, public recognition was limited, but generations later they are well-known. Some revelation and mysteries are LOCKED UP... or held up UNTIL ITS DESIGNATED TIME OF RELEASE. Many of God's people are writing "outside of their time." I have been told many times that I am "ahead of my timing" … but the truth is this: Some messages are released "at an appointed time" and then incubates in its present state until the day of its FULFILLMENT. Its role in the incubation period is to release FAITH AND HOPE concerning what God has promised. In addition, other messages BUILD UPON it… rely upon it… rest in anticipation of it. Truly this is the case for **Isaiah 7:14** and **Habakkuk 2:1-3.**

Elliot's Commentary for English Readers conveys the reference to the "appointed time" in Habakkuk as meaning that the revelation "pants for the day of completion, which shall do it justice. It longs to fulfill its destiny."[34] I love the use of the phrase "pants for its day of completion" here. It literally indicates that the word God releases "longs" to complete its ordained purpose. How phenomenal is that – especially when it is a beautiful promise!

I hear this prophetic word for someone right now: "Many of my scribes have penned instruction that has not been well received in this generation, says the Spirit of the Lord. There is coming a time when I will pour rain on their Words and send it into the ears of my people. What is seen as none sense in your inkwell will become rhema in due season."

People of God, revelation WAITS to come forth like an infant in the womb. It does not linger or prolong itself. **It never delays.** It incubates and WAITS to burst forth. For some of you, this will really bear witness with your Spirit. The revelation you received is NOT outside of time or ahead of your time. It is RIGHT ON TIME… for its appointed time.

If this stood as truth for Habakkuk, the prophets of old and other great people in antiquity, it is clearly a word of truth for us in present day. Our hearts must grow in patience even if it is a patience that extends beyond

---

[34] Bible Hub, *Elliot's Commentary for English Readers: Habakkuk*, http://biblehub.com/commentaries/ellicott/habakkuk/2.htm

our capacity to understand *or even our lifetime in the earth.* Many of us may not realize this, but there is honor is being remembered. In no way am I indicating that we should think small or not expect great works! Rather, I am encouraging every prophetic scribe to abandon any and all selfish ambition and earnestly seek God's will. Scribes? Be ready. Be found with oil in your lamp at THE appointed time for *you.*

Remember, an entire generation missed God in the Old Covenant… and failed to enter the Promised Land. Many people in scripture faced detours they were never able to make a comeback. Destiny and purpose is locked up in you for yourself and for others.

ALL THINGS NEW

Then He who sat on the throne said, "Behold, I make all things new." And He said to me, "Write, for these words are true and faithful."
~ Revelation 21:5

YOUR NEW DAY

Prophetic scribes, we are in a New Day. In this age, we are flooded with endless information concerning every topic imaginable. And, the information – both good and bad - is readily available without hindrance. At times, the voice of the stranger *seems* to overtake the voice of the Lord. Without a solid understanding of the Word and maturing, PROGRESSIVE discernment, one can barely distinguish between echoes, soul revelation, angry voices, clairvoyance, the soul and the voice of the Good Shepherd.

Many prophetic scribes are being raised up in this hour to strengthen the people of God in their discernment. I firmly believe that we are God's secret weapons in the 21st Century – that army of scribes whom He has raised up and positioned in the very fabric of our congregation to amplify and solidify His Word. As part of this New Day, the dream realm is rising among the faithful as a tool to filter out the false voices. This is why must stay *in the* Word, remain rooted in prayer and pursue a submitted life in Christ.

In both the Old and New Covenants, only "certain men" had strategic access to this realm: Daniel **(Daniel 7:1)**; Apostle John **(The Book of Revelation)**; Habakkuk **(Habakkuk 1:1; 2:1-3)**; Solomon **(1 Kings 3:1-5)**; and the man clothed in linen from **Ezekiel 9 & 10**. Their scribal realms were STRIKINGLY DISTINCT. However, when you examine their lives prior to the access they were given, you will discover that their alignment with God was extreme, sure… apostolic! They did not make God casual… approaching His throne any old kind of way. Reverence was critical to their journey! Many scribes today claim to be prophetic but they lack reverence for God! They will write, record and demonstrate ANYTHING and attach his name to it, and boast that He gave it to them. Help us Father! They were not living on a salvation rollercoaster, drawing the grace card by convenience. They sought vicariously to be rooted and grounded in love, trust and hope!

- Daniel was so sensitive to the spirit that he fell on his face at the sound of God's voice.

- The Apostle John was overwhelmed at receiving a Revelation of Jesus Christ.

- Habakkuk was determined to prove the goodness of the God he faithfully served.

- The man clothed in linen had an opportunity to touch the glory of God.

I am reminded of an encounter God had with Solomon, the son of King David, in the **scribal** realm of dreams and visions. **1 Kings 3:5** NIV says, *"At Gibeon **the Lord appeared to Solomon** during the night**_in a dream,_** and God said, Ask for whatever you want me to give you."*

I have never experienced this particular *type* of encounter in a dream. However, I have had encounters in which a series of doors were open to me, each containing varying treasures and I could *choose* what I wanted. I've since learned that this is quite common in the dream realm. I do not believe, however, that many dreamers have understood the "weight" of that specific type of dream interaction. Think about it? The difference between the dream types is quite obvious. In Solomon's meeting, God asked him directly what he wanted without presenting anything before him directly. In the dream with the doors, the rooms already contained specific types of treasure that could be chosen. The significance is this: Our interaction with God in the dream realm is not based SOLELY on interpreting what we see or receiving what we need. We are also presented with opportunities to access our *righteous heart's* desire. Thinking this way, however, requires that we accept a fresh, new supernatural reality surrounding dreams and visions: We can seek to deliberately interact with Him. (I am not talking about controlling dreams here. We do not have that kind of power or authority. God is in control of the dream realm. Let's be clear. Rather, we can prepare ourselves to be sensitive to the opportunities in our dream realm in which He has ordained us to interact with Him.)

Solomon's response to God's request was immediate, bold and in the form of a prayer. In it, He spent time thanking God... extending that gratefulness. In addition, he did not to ask for fame or riches, but for guidance to manage his inherited Kingdom. He wasn't thinking about himself, but about the wisdom needed to be a righteous king to the people who needed him. **Solomon wanted to rule well.**

He responded to God like this in **vs. 7-9:** *"Now, Lord my God, you have made your servant king in place of my father David. But I am only a little child and do not know how to carry out my duties. Your servant is here among the people you have chosen, a great people, too numerous to count or number. So give your servant a discerning heart to govern your people and to distinguish between right and wrong. For who is able to govern this great people of yours?"*

God not only granted Solomon's desires for wisdom, but gave him more than he could have imagined.

In **v. 12-14** God says to him: ***"I will do what you have asked.*** *I will give you a wise and discerning heart, so that there will never have been anyone like you, nor will there ever be.* ***Moreover, I will give you what you have not asked for***—*both wealth and honor*—*so that in your lifetime you will have no equal among kings. And if you walk in obedience to me and keep my decrees and commands as David your father did, I will give you a long life."*

In Solomon's dream realm, God:

- Requested something from Solomon.

- Waited for Solomon to respond.

- Listened to Solomon's detailed response.

- Received Solomon's request.

- Agreed to do what **Solomon** asked.

- Gave Solomon a wise a discerning heart, which released him into the office of a scribe where he could rightly judge the affairs in the Kingdom.

- Saturated Solomon in the scribal anointing or the scribe's anointing; and positioned him as the greatest scribe and sage of his time, of which no other has ever compared.

- Gave him wealth and honor beyond that of any king.

- Caused him to live in an exclusively privileged realm as a King in which He had no equal.

- Promised him long life if he remained obedient after the pattern of His father David.

Scribes of the King! Look at what took place in this specific dream encounter. Solomon had God with God as a child! His conversation and interaction with God wasn't simply a passing dream, but a very real encounter. I firmly believe that the Lord wants to bring each one of us into this place in our NEW DAY! He is taking us out of this world and into His court where we are able to interact with Him as sons in a way in which many of us may have never experienced before.

Listen, we know this was a "scribal realm" because of the type of impartation that took place; and by watching the kind of fruit that came out of that impartation that enabled Solomon to strengthen his administration, serve as a judge in the midst of disputes, serve as a counselor regarding life issues, record uncommon songs and proverbs, understand nature and the ways of animals, and so much more. **Solomon teaches us that in the scribal realm, we are able to uncover treasures about ANYTHING – not just spiritual things.** He assists us in seeing that revelation is not limited to prophecy; but that it really does encompass a broad expanse of knowledge and ideas.

1 Kings 4:29-34 NIV reveal that Solomon was walking in *"wisdom and very great insight, and a breadth of understanding as measureless as the sand on the seashore. Solomon's wisdom was greater than the wisdom of all the people of the East, and greater than all the wisdom of Egypt. He was wiser than anyone else, including Ethan the Ezrahite—wiser than Heman, Kalkol and Darda, the sons of Mahol. And his fame spread to all the surrounding nations. **He spoke three thousand proverbs and his songs numbered a thousand and five.** He spoke about plant life, from the cedar of Lebanon to the hyssop that grows out of walls. He also spoke about animals and birds, reptiles and fish. From all nations people came to listen to Solomon's wisdom, sent by all the kings of the world, who had heard of his wisdom."*

People of God, really look at what TOOK PLACE in this dream! Solomon's dream encounter released an impartation that GREW UP in him. It was so great that his impact crossed thousands of years; and his scribal fruit saturates our faith today. Then consider Habakkuk, who was able to retrieve an oracle of such significance that it is still speaking into

135

the hearts of those that have caught the vision. **What once-in-a-lifetime-type-of-treasure could there be in your scribal realm?**

Is there a message Father longs to release through you that is critical for the generations to come? Are there questions He desires to ask that will give birth to your destiny? Are there prayers you will pray in your dreams that will release the hosts of heaven on your behalf, on behalf of others? Are there people you will meet supernaturally in the dream realm, that God will bring into your life at a later time like Anais and Paul? Are you prepared for your New Day as a dreamer?

PREPARING FOR THE NEW DAY

Is it possible to prepare one's self to enter the realm of dreams and visions? Yes, it is! Unfortunately, many prophetic people whom I encounter spend their supernatural lives waiting for prophecies and dreams to supernaturally visit them. So many people "wait on Go" as in hanging around hoping that He will stop in to speak to them "if it is His will." Listen, if the scriptures tell us nothing else… they convey that God has a great love for us… one in which He longs to be one with us. He even promises that that He will not withhold one single from those who belong to Him. People of God, there is no limitations on the depths of His goodness toward us. Our expectation must increase. The New Day requires that we live in expectancy, preparedness and **deliberate** pursuit. We must pant for, long after, thirst for… the presence of the Father. Of all the lessons we have learned from Habakkuk so far, these three areas are what I call "the keys" to embracing the New Day for *the dreamer*.

KEY OF EXPECTANCY

Psalm 62:5 AMP says, *"For God alone my soul waits in silence and quietly submits to Him, for my hope is from Him."*

Expectancy is standing in expectations of the greatest possible outcome in a circumstance or even as it relates to a person. In scripture, I equate this in living in a place of continuous HOPE in Christ. The Greek word for hope is translated *elpis* and it is used 54 times in the 1769 King James Version of the Bible. It is often associated with the word faith, and its relationship toward the importance of trusting the Lord. **It is a word that that ushers us to _anticipate_ God's goodness, his promises with unwavering confidence.**

In short, we can see expectancy as ANTICIPATION. In the context of our teaching, we should EXPECT God to meet us supernaturally in our dreams and visions.

God will indeed meet us at will; but He has also given us common sense concerning how to prepare for that meeting. In the 21st Century, I believe it is imperative for the present day scribe (or any son of God for that matter) to be proactive in every aspect of their relationship with God. As supernatural people, we should prepare ourselves to already be in a position to fully receive the Lord.

KEY OF PREPARATION

Matthew 24:44 KJV says, *"Therefore be ye also ready: for in such an hour as ye think not the Son of man cometh."*

Yes, I know this scripture is about the return of the Lord. And yes, there are other scriptures I could use here but I love how direct it is in conveying this sentiment: "BE READY!" In other words, be prepared. Preparation for the dreamer includes some very special and unique aspects. I want to take a few minutes to look at these.

Some years ago, I spent a lot of time complaining that the Lord had stopped visiting me through dreams. My heart was so heavy over this season in my

137 of this season in my

137

life that I actually became angry, frustrated and upset. One day, as I wept over this… I heard Father say, "If you would just go to bed at a decent time, I would have time to visit you in deep sleep." I was convicted… and crushed! I realized it wasn't that the Lord did not desire to visit me through dreams… I was not preparing myself to receive them. There I was in all my selfishness… being found without my oil.

You see, preparation is indeed spiritual. We've already covered many of those spiritual things. But there are also some practical things we need to consider like *rest and sleep*. Seriously. Neglecting these two areas could very will hinder or even block the depth of your dream realm encounters. Prophetic scribes, I know what it is like to be tired and what is means to be exhausted. They are not the same!

To be tired can refer to being weary or having a need for rest. Most of us experience this at least weekly. We generally go take a nap or get a good night's rest and we are good to go. Exhaustion is something entirely different as it relates not only to a physical tiredness, but a spiritual and mental one as well. In my household, when I am exhausted… I literally pass out once my head hits the pillow and quite honestly, that's not sleep! Your body and mind are literally in shut down mode.

Honestly answer this question: "Is this how to present our body as a living sacrifice?" Whether tired or exhausted, being unprepared is the same. For the dreamer, this is a critical reality check. I had to confess to that I was not just tired during this season of my life, but exhausted. I needed to realign my life in such a way that I did not "neglect" what God had for me. Sometimes, we have life issues beyond our control that places us in a position to be tired or exhausted. However, I believe most of us simply suffer from doing to many things in our own strength surrounded by a lack of PREPARATION.

Psalm 127:2 AMP says, *"It is <u>vain</u> for you to rise up early, to sit up late, to eat the bread of sorrows: for so he giveth his beloved sleep."*

Let that passage soak in.

We must begin to see sleep as a GIFT... not as a necessity! Not only is our Father the dream giver; but He also created sleep for us as a GIFT. I'm going to stop right there, throw down the mic and SHOUT over this! Oh how precious is our rest, relaxation, DEEP SLEEP AND SLUMBER IS TO GOD! Neglecting this area of our lives closes the door to more than we have probably ever realized. If we are too exhausted to receive a night vision, there is no way we can properly and thoroughly process visions while awake. We've got to do better. Taking the scribal realm of dreams and visions requires facing this reality.

We need to confess our sin of neglect in this area to God, and trust Holy Spirit in guiding us in developing an earnest plan to get ourselves back on track. In fact, I have a study guide and worksheet online at The Scribal Realm website to help bring breakthrough in this area. As believers, we know that this issue involves a holistic perspective as well (eating right, exercise, etc.).

Daniel was a fit dreamer! He was clear in His mind, body and spirit.

My first step was simple. I had to learn how to power down and relax from the overwhelming days and weeks I would have. Whether that power-down began with sipping hot tea for 15 minutes (in complete silence) after arriving home for the evening or taking a few minutes to play my favorite, soothing instrumental music and stretching out in my prayer room. I also learned to de-stress just before bed by soaking 30 minutes or so in aromatic bath salts in a hot tub set candle light. This might not sound like much, but it worked wonders for me. I was able to lay down in my bed and actually fall asleep. In addition, I took the necessary steps to set my own bedtime...

turning my 5 hours of sleep nightly into about 7 hours at least five times a week. The National Sleep Foundation suggests that the average person between 26 and 65 years old receive between 7 and 9 hours of sleep.[35] Remember, entering into this NEW DAY requires completely changing how we choose to view and approach the scribal realm of dreams and visions.

KEY OF PURSUIT

Many of us understand what it means to pursue God, meaning follow-after His presence with urgency and great zeal with our whole heart. We must see the desire to dream and see visions as part of this pursuit. The outcome of dreaming is that we might have revelation knowledge and insight, knowing what is the present and perfect will of God. Further, it is the desire to share what is revealed to us with others… that their eyes might be opened to the revelation of Christ; and hearts filled with His great love. All roads of pursuit lead back to God, and his reconciliation plan.

Prepared dreamers are proactive dreamers.

The Apostle James taught us how to cry out for wisdom in the midst of trials and tribulations. Yet, we know inwardly that this cry for wisdom is not simply for times of trouble. It should be for everyday living and development. As scribes who dream at a high capacity, we should long for interactions in the dream realm, especially since our perspective on its uniqueness to our calling has been revealed. In this New Day, we are being urged to recognize it as an incubator and conduit of the eternal wisdom of God.

James 1:5-6 NIV says, *"If any of you lacks wisdom, he should ask God, who gives generously to all without finding fault, and it will be given to*

---

[35] National Sleep Foundation, Recommended Sleep Chart, https://sleepfoundation.org/how-sleep-works/how-much-sleep-do-we-really-need

him. But _he must ask in faith,_ **without doubting,** _because he who doubts is like a wave of the sea, blown and tossed by the wind.…"_

Our pursuit is not meant to be another place of work and toil, but a place of existence and being. Pursuit is a posture, not a series of works. It's as simply as praying: Father, speak to me in my dreams. Habakkuk showed us what this looked like in his own life. He said he would stand on his rampart which came naturally to him, and "look to see" what God would say to him. Scribes, it's time to unlock this key and respond accordingly.

IMPACTING THE NEW DAY

Mark 12:30-31 NIV, _"Love the Lord your God with all your heart and with all your soul and with all your mind and with all your strength.'[a] The second is this: 'Love your neighbor as yourself.' There is no commandment greater than these."_

No man is an island.

We were not created to dwell in solitude, void of interacting with and impacting one another. The very nature of humanity, as God alone intended it, requires interdependency – iron sharpening iron.

We are **intricately and irrefutably** bound to one another in God's love and Christ's defined concept of brotherhood. In this season of my life, I have come to grasp this truth as a core belief in a way that I never have before. I see everything that we complete or accomplish in service to our Father from the perspective of interacting with or impacting people for His Glory. It keeps me grounded, and focused on the eternal message of reconciliation and the greatest commandment (Mark 12:30-31). Scribes, my intent here is not to preach at you… but to really press Father's heart into you. We must constantly be reminded that God's first love is us… people; and in turn, we must seek out the compassion of Christ in our own

141

hearts! It is for this reason that I constantly encourage scribes to walk in deep, intimate understanding of "The Scribal Anointing®," fully grasping what it means to live one's life as a scribe INSTRUCTED in the Kingdom of heaven. What we produce for public consumption and what we speak through our intimate lives *is not and never will be* just about US – our vision, plans, personal dreams and goals, but about souls, generations.

I want to leave you with an understanding of this truth: <u>Every</u> book, play, skit, song, poem, grant, letter, etc. that is prophetically released **to you** is an assignment for *someone* else somewhere. When you write, record or demonstrate it, there are souls in the earth who are a destined over the course of time to run into that assignment by God's design.

Pause here for a moment.

Habakkuk did not know that his experiences in writing God's oracle would impact my life at this level. The original writers of the Bible did not have you "specifically" in mind when they were prophetically inspired to write and record the scriptures. YET, here we are… every day… walking out and living by the plethora of wisdom we have gleaned not only from their written inspiration, but from the history of their experiences!

For me, I am unable to get caught up in the hype of being a best-selling author or being the guru of this or that. There is absolutely nothing… and I mean NOTHING wrong with being the recipient of God's favor in this area as a scribe. HOWEVER, if you stand like Habakkuk and don't see "this kind" of return in your life-time – IT IS OKAY. Remember, Habakkuk never… never… ever got to reach His audience in any tangible direct way. Yes, I know I've said that a hundred times already. But look at the fruit that came from that "necessary and critical oracle" in Habakkuk 2. Our spiritual lives are transformed by that one revelation of God. Wow!

What if you have spent years of research, tons of money and countless hours to develop that ONE essential revelation God gave you in the scribal realm of dreams and visions... and only ONE PERSON – from your perspective – seems to have gotten it, are you a failure? By Kingdom standards absolutely not! Perhaps that revelation was for that "one person" to catch it and, in turn, run and make that revelation famous. Paul took Habakkuk's understanding of "the just shall live by faith" and expounded on it in a way that has brought many believers across time into great understanding. WHAT IF... Habakkuk had never penned that Holy Spirit inspired phrase within the context of his journey? Paul, in all honesty, may have never been empowered to expound upon its meaning.

Let me bring this message home to you.

Earlier, I shared concerning one of the most challenging crises I have ever faced in ministry. I loved the Lord, and would never abandon my relationship with Him... but I was done with people and the institution of religion. I was so devastated by this situation that I did not think I could recover enough to continue in scribal ministry or lead people. I just wanted to love God and never, ever deal with Christians or the religion of Christianity again. I literally walked away from ministry, relationships... and nearly lost my family in the process as I muddled through. This was a big deal since I am known to be faithful to relationships, always wanting to work things out whenever possible. One of the scribes I raised up said to me, *"You can't give up. We need you."* Although I was empty, and really void of life... I did what I call "sustaining ministry"- *only* what was necessary to keep going out of obligation, not passion or desire. I was going through the motions.

One day, while sitting in my prayer room crying... and pleading with Father to take my pain away I was drawn to pull some books from my bookshelf. These three books, by the way, were given to me several years before when I was a baby believer (less than a year in the faith). They were still encased in plastic wrap like the day they came out of the box. I peeled

143

back the plastic, and picked up this one particular book on spiritual warfare. I figured now was as good a time as any to read it. I needed some relief! It was a very unattractive book. It had a brown cover, brown lettering on the front in big letters… and the author's name. I would never, ever have purchased it on my own. I opened it up and began to read the first few pages.

In it was a prophecy, and the prophecy said something like this (and I paraphrase): "In this coming season, God is raising an uncommon army. They will be an army of writers unlike any that have come before…." As I read this prophetic word, a deep guttural cry emerged from me. I could do nothing but let the words of that book *heal* my soul. There was so much detail in this prophecy that it literally GAVE ME a reason to go on, a reason to live… a reason to believe that this strange and weird ministry wasn't a waste of my time.

In that moment I realized this supernatural truth: That book was assigned to me. *I was assigned to that book… and despite where I was or what was going on with me… I was able to connect with my destiny and purpose because the author was OBEDIENT to write it.* God used it to affirm a calling on my life that no man had ever been able to articulate or even comprehend. It was what I needed to continue my journey.

She never knew me. I tried to reach out to her; but she would pass away before we could meet so I said my thank yous to God. The prophecy from that book changed my life.

Scribes, listen to this. The book was written in 1980. I was probably in the 3rd or 4th grade at that time… and had no real knowledge of God. It would be two decades later before I would ever come to know Christ as my deliverer… and another five before I would receive the Word of the Lord to build His scribal army. It would be four years after that before I opened the pages of this book… solely at the leading of Holy Spirit! Nearly 30 years had passed since this woman wrote that book and I came to encounter it! This was NOT a coincidence. Sometimes, I wonder where I would be if not for the obedience of that prophetic scribe all those years ago. Her message was TRULY for me… in that moment in time.

She wasn't famous. She wasn't a notable New York Time's Best Seller. She wasn't a celebrity minister or Pulitzer Prize winning author. She was never picked up by a traditional publishing company. Yet, her books are preserved by random people all over the web who felt an urgency to carry what this powerful prophet poured out to the nations. Even now, other scribes preserve her legacy. That message, though she is with the Lord, is continuing to be propelled in the earth impacting countless others – influencing leaders.

Now, I want to give you one more example.

About six years ago (maybe longer), I began a deliberate quest to learn everything I could about apostolic ministry. Unfortunately, the classes, workshops and resources I had were very elementary and didn't address the depths of the subject matter that I needed. I was desperate to understand the calling on my life for season that I was walking in. While watching a movie on the web one day, I decided to search one more time…. and this book popped up in the first three searches. If I remember correctly, it was number one. I proceeded to read about the book online, and I placed an order on the web. Then, I decided to look up the author. Let me tell you, I spent the next three hours reading the articles on the website, watching videos, and examining the other books that were made available. I was BLOWN AWAY! This particular author had answers to _every single question_ I had been asking about myself. What was even more amazing was that she lived right here in Georgia.

Immediately, I was moved to contact her. Never in my entire life have I pursued a minister or a ministry for anything! I am not easily impressed by people and have no interest in falling into celebrity preacher worship, and spazzing out as a revelation-junkie. Holy Spirit in me was ON FIRE! I could feel it! And today, because of that book… the articles on the website and the videos that were obediently released, we walk in covenant today. We were always meant to connect and be an intimate part of one another's lives. This isn't just super spiritual talk! The connection itself has brought undeniable, unquestioning and instantaneous IMPACT, HEALING & DELIVERANCE into my life! My very soul has been propelled to greatness, in the same way, in my opinion as the disciples were launched through relationship with Christ. I have sense developed a very unique understanding of true apostolic authority and mentorship. In my entire walk with the Lord I can only pinpoint three… maybe four instances of something this significant happening to me in my spiritual life… all linked to books.

Scribes of the King, who is waiting on you?

God told Abraham that if He found just one righteous soul in the midst of Sodom and Gomorrah He would save the city! Just one. If no one else got anything from the books and messages released by the authors I mentioned, I did! Your prophetic book, song, play, skit, grant, letter, devotion, poem, etc. is worth writing, recording, demonstrating and publishing EVEN IF only one person has the opportunity to hear it! What if that one person is destined to raise up a NATION! What if that one person grabs hold of that message and changes the course of their future lineage! What if that one person becomes the vessel God uses to build upon the revelation you received… in such a way that it transcends cultures, nations?

What if the keys to someone's New Day are in your belly? I know the keys to my New Day were in the hands of the author's I encountered. And their messages impacted my life at a level that never would have occurred without their labor. To understand this is to grasp the reality of how God created us to prophetically interact with one another in the Kingdom. There are many prophetic writers who are now in the presence of the Lord who NEVER saw the success or the mass distribution of their books; but stand today as patriarchs and matriarchs among us. Prophetic scribes, what you have in your hand has the potential to forge a NEW DAY.

The New Day isn't necessarily depended on a calendar year, date or time. It is about releasing the message that will push others into "their" New Day – new ways of thinking, existing, being, relating and understanding. It is about preparing the way for them to better understand and know the works, ways, and worship of God. You have one role in the Kingdom: *Walk in obedience to the Father in everything He commands.* And again, I ask: "How will you respond to what God has revealed in this book?"

HOW WILL YOU RESPOND?

When Abram received the command from God to leave Ur, he immediately gathered his family, all their possessions and departed. No hesitation. When Mary learned that she would carry the Christ, she responded: "Be it unto me." When Christ was faced with the reality of His calling in the Garden, He declared: "Not my will, but your will be done."

In every situation there was a call and a response. Responding means to reply with an answer, reaction or action to a question asked or a situation presented. In light of this discussion, it is referring to the action *you* plan to take after *receiving* what Father has revealed in this book. How will you respond to God's request to answer the deeper calling to the scribal realm of dreams and visions? What is your natural and spiritual answer to this question?

I tell you, there's no reason why any prophetic scribe who dreams should remain in the shallow waters of the dream realm at this point. Either the message in this book will be ridiculous and a bunch of non-sense to those who read it or it will be extremely affirming and challenging – putting those who long to be better stewards over their own supernatural realm of dreams and visions in a position to grow exponentially.

I suffered for years in the midst of my scribal calling – silently. I sought to understand who I was with no example standing before me, no pattern to follow, no script to imitate and no understanding of what I was doing. I was laughed at, discounted… excluded, seen as weird… and probably accused of things I don't even know about. All I know is that my desire to obey God pushed me past all the hang ups, fears and confusion. My desire to please God became greater than any personal aspiration, triumph or belief. I said to myself over and over again, "I would do this just for one person if I had too." I realize today that *I had to* walk this way. I learned from Apostle Joseph Prude that "anytime you are the progenitor of a thing… you are the one that has to clear the land, plow the ground and till the fields. You have to get dirty, bloody and beat up. But guess what, it will be worth it." Scribes of the King, you don't have to clear the land, plow the ground or till the fields in this area. It has been done for you. The architectural plans have been given. You simply have to be obedient to build! You can glean from the wisdom that is now available in this area of ministry through this resource and other resources that have been made available. Say YES to Him. Allow Holy Spirit to rebuild your understanding of dreams and visions, being *ever mindful* of the "Dream Safeguards" we covered.

Habakkuk's response was simple. He said I will "look to see what you will say to me and what answer I am to give." When God replied to him, he responded by following his instructions EXACTLY and as you know the rest is *His-story*. Hold on to this affirming passage:

Hebrews 1:1-3, 13-14 AMP says this: *"Now faith is the assurance (title deed, confirmation) of things hoped for (divinely guaranteed), and the evidence of things not seen [the conviction of their reality—faith comprehends as fact what cannot be experienced by the physical senses].*

For by this [kind of] faith the men of old gained [divine] approval. By faith [that is, with an inherent trust and enduring confidence in the power, wisdom and goodness of God] we understand that the worlds (universe, ages) were framed and created [formed, put in order, and equipped for their intended purpose] by the word of God, so that what is seen was not made out of things which are visible."

Embrace your New Day.

I'M PRAYING FOR YOU

Prophetic Scribes, agree with me:

F ather, I thank you for this New Day you have presented before your **Matthew 13:52** prophetic scribes. I thank you that you are affirming them in their calling into the office of the scribe, and as scribes who dream dreams and see visions. I thank you for taking away any doubt or fears concerning embracing the scribal realm of dreams and visions as they walk hand-in-hand with Holy Spirit.

Detox your sons from everything they have been taught, everything they have believed and everything they have thought concerning the ministry of the scribe, the prophetic scribe, The Scribal Anointing and the scribal realm of dreams and visions that stands in conflict with your Word. Father, I thank you that as you bring them into this fresh revelation that you continue breaking any alliances with religion, legalism, witchcraft or other occult activities that prevent them from walking in a pure understanding of the prophetic. Expose, break and uproot any areas of self-sabotage, slothfulness, procrastination, laziness, bitterness toward the prophetic and any other bitter fruit from their lives. Father, I stand with them for any times in which they have declared false dreams and false visions; and despised prophecy. I stand in repentance with them right now. Cause them to move out of the past and into your New Day where they will see, hear, comprehend, record, write and release what you have given to them.

Give them wisdom in identifying their rampart. Give them wisdom in standing on their rampart to look to see what you will say. Give them wisdom in recognizing and discerning what answer they are to give. Strengthen them in writing the vision, making it plain on the tablets. Open their hearts, mind and eyes to receive what it means to live and exist in "the scribal realm" in both the spirit and the natural. Cause them to experience what it means to dream differently and deeper as scribes. Help them identify their oracle and burden in this hour. Help them stand in strength on their scribal prayer watch.

Rebuild, restructure and reinforce their trust in the dream realm. Give them the wisdom to identify and establish their scribal atmosphere and uncover the treasures you have assigned to them. Cause them to recognize and take hold of their specific scribal realm. I declare that they will embrace their New Day. They will move from milk to meat in understanding their calling and purpose. They will become master writers and recorders, faithful to pick up their stylus and write or record when you summon them. I declare that they walk under The Scribal Anointing® after the pattern of Ezra.

Help them Father, see the significance of the calling of the prophetic scribe upon their lives. Cause them to hunger and thirst after you in the midst of their calling like never before. I pray that they are sensitive and responsive to Holy Spirit and able to properly digest all that they have learned and apply it as it is brought into their remembrance and made plain. Reinforce their desire to make you known in the earth and to see souls reconciled with Christ. Father, I pray that they do not miss the appointed times set for them. Holy Spirit, teach them to govern the scribal realm of dreams and visions according to their portion – never comparting, competing or compromising in the midst of their calling. Remind them Father, that Christ did not come to entertain us but to set the captives free. Strengthen this uncommon, strategic, prophetic scribal nation. In Jesus Christ's name. Amen.

MEET THERESA HARVARD JOHNSON

Theresa Harvard Johnson is best known for her revelatory insight, understanding and apostolic teachings surrounding the ministry of the prophetic scribe and prophetic writing. She has published, contributed to or co-authored more than 14 books including her signature publication, *"The Scribal Anointing: Scribes Instructed in the Kingdom of Heaven,"* which has been taught world-wide. Walking under a heavy apostolic mandate, Theresa has an intense desire to see the ministry of the prophetic scribe fully restored within the congregation, particularly as it relates to those scribes destined to lead at a global capacity in government, education, worship and the arts. At the heart of this call is a *fiery and fierce* passion to see every believer come to know, understand and embrace this high calling.

Available Books:
- Writing & the Prophetic
- The Scribal Realm of Dreams & Visions
- The Scribal Realm Companion (Dream & Impact Journal)
- The Scribal Anointing: Scribes Instructed in the Kingdom of Heaven
- The Scribal Companion Student Workbook
- Scribal Purpose: 10 Reasons Why God Has Called You to Write
- Spiritual Critiquing Literary Works
- Literary Evangelism Beyond the Open Mic
- The Sin of Spiritual Plagiarism: Unauthorized Vessels

- 40 Signs of a Prophetic Scribe
- Signs of a Scribal Prophet
- 50 Indisputable Biblical Facts About the Ministry of the Prophetic Scribe

*Books are available on Amazon.com & The Book Patch.

Email: dreamencounter@thescribalrealm.com
Join Our Dream Community: thescribalrealm.com
School: schoolofthescribe.com

Made in the USA
Columbia, SC
13 March 2022